STORIES FROM WEST VIRGINIA'S CIVIL RIGHTS HISTORY

STORIES FROM WEST VIRGINIA'S CIVIL RIGHTS HISTORY

A NEW HOME FOR LIBERTY

J.R. CLIFFORD AND THE CARRIE WILLIAMS CASE

BY THOMAS W. RODD

Charleston, West Virginia

Quarrier Press
Charleston, WV

Copyright 2015, Thomas W. Rodd

All rights reserved. No part of this book may be reproduced in any form or means, electronic or mechanical, including photocopying, recording, or by any information storage and retrieval system, without permission in writing from the publisher.

cover design: Brandae Mullins
book design: Megan Knight

ISBN 10: 1-942294-03-4
ISBN 13: 978-1-942294-03-0

Library of Congress Control Number: 2015939613

10 9 8 7 6 5 4 3 2 1

Cover photos, clockwise:
J. R. Clifford, Granville Hall, and Carrie Williams

Printed in the United States of America

Distributed by:

West Virginia Book Co.
1125 Central Ave.
Charleston, WV 25302
www.wvbookco.com

TABLE OF CONTENTS

Introduction . . . vii

A New Home For Liberty . . . 1

J. R. Williams and the Carrie Williams Case . . . 33

Appendices . . . 78

    Historical Accuracy, Sources and Credits . . . 78

    Questions for Critical Thinking and Discussion . . . 82

    Words and Terms . . . 84

    A Timeline of Events In the Life of J.R. Clifford . . . 86

    Timeline of West Virginia Statehood . . . 88

    Text of the West Virginia Supreme Court Opinion In the Carrie Williams Case . . . 89

    Abraham Lincoln on the Admission of West Virginia . . . 94

    Bibliography . . . 97

About the Author . . . 101

DEDICATION

For Judy

INTRODUCTION

The State of West Virginia has a unique history, and these stories show how special and important that history is.

In 1861, the State of Virginia's government decided to secede from the United States of America in order to be part of a new country, the Confederacy, where slavery would be protected. The Civil War began when the United States government would not allow this to happen.

Many white people in Virginia, especially in the West, did not want to leave the United States. And of course, almost all black Virginians, most of whom were slaves and none of whom could vote, were also opposed to secession.

When the Civil War began, leaders in Western Virginia formed a new state out of part of Virginia, hoping to remain part of the United States, no matter how the Civil War turned out. As we now know, the Confederacy failed in its effort and Virginia remained in the Union—but now with a new sister State of West Virginia.

Brave people, young and old, who believed in liberty and justice for all no matter the color of a person's skin, are an important part of West Virginia's and America's history. These people—like J.R. Clifford, Granville Hall, and Carrie Williams—are role models for all of us. It is an honor and privilege to tell their stories.

We hope you enjoy this book!

-Tom Rodd

Stories from West Virginia's Civil Rights History

"A NEW HOME FOR LIBERTY"
BY THOMAS RODD

CHAPTER ONE

Parkersburg, West Virginia, 1913

It was a summer day in 1913. The broad Ohio River flowed lazily beside the Parkersburg, West Virginia railroad station. A breeze on the water formed ripples that sparkled with golden sunlight.

Two children were playing in the honeysuckle vines that grew beside the station platform. The children's names were Deborah and Joshua Hall. Deborah was fourteen years old; Joshua was age twelve.

Granville Hall, the children's grandfather, stood on the platform looking down at his grandchildren.

Granville wore a white linen suit and a broad-brimmed straw hat. He had just had a trim in the station barbershop, and his cheeks were still pink from the hot towels.

Deborah reached up and held out a white blossom to her grandfather.

Granville Hall

"Grandpa," she said, "these flowers smell wonderful!"

Granville took the flower, and inhaled its sweet, spicy scent.

"They certainly are wonderful," he said. "Honeysuckle is one of my favorites."

*   *   *   *   *

A distant whistle grew louder and louder—then, with a "screech" of brakes and a cloud of smoke, a five-car passenger train arrived at the station.

A tall man stepped down from the train. He wore a grey suit and brown hat and tie, and his white hair and moustache stood out against his brown skin.

He was followed by a young woman wearing a long grey skirt and blouse, and a white hat trimmed with a yellow ribbon.

The baggage room door of the station building opened. A railroad porter carrying a suitcase came onto the platform. "Paging Mr. Granville Hall!" the porter called. "Paging Mr. Granville Hall!"

"Here," Granville said. "Here! I'm Granville Hall!"

The porter carried the suitcase down the platform. "Mr. Hall," he said, "the hotel finally delivered your baggage."

"Thank you very much," Granville said. He took the bag and gave the porter a tip.

The tall man who had just stepped down from the train walked a few steps across the platform and addressed Granville.

"Excuse me, sir," said the man. "I just overheard that porter call out your name. Are you the same Granville Hall who was West Virginia's Secretary of State—it must be fifty years ago?"

"Yes," said Granville, "I am that Granville Hall. But I am afraid you have me at a disadvantage. Have we met before?"

"No, I don't believe we've met before," the man replied, "but I know my West Virginia history. You were also the reporter at the Wheeling Statehood Convention—and a passionate advocate for our new State of West Virginia. Am I correct?"

"Why, yes, I was," said Granville. "And I still have passionate feelings about our new State." He extended his hand. "May I make your acquaintance?"

"Mr. Hall," the man replied, "my name is John Robert Clifford."

"Most people call me 'J.R.'" he continued. "I am an attorney and a publisher in Martinsburg, West Virginia. I am traveling with my daughter, Miss Mary Clifford—we have come to Parkersburg for a political meeting."

The men shook hands. Mary Clifford, the young woman in the yellow hat, also shook hands with Granville.

John Robert Clifford

Mary Clifford

Granville turned to his grandchildren, who had climbed onto the platform and were brushing honeysuckle leaves off their clothes.

"These are my grandchildren, Deborah and Joshua," Granville said. "We are taking a train to the West Virginia Day celebrations in Clarksburg." The children shook hands with J.R. and Mary.

"Mary," said J.R. to his daughter, "Fifty years ago, Mr. Hall was at the center of a world-changing struggle—the creation of West Virginia. He witnessed all of the ins and outs of that historic battle."

"But Mr. Hall," said Mary, "you must have been so young."

"Not too young," Granville said. "I was born in 1837, and I had just turned twenty-four when I started working at the Convention in Wheeling."

"How about you, Dad?" asked Mary. "How old were you when West Virginia was created?"

"I was born in 1848," said J.R., "and I was 15 in 1863, when President Lincoln signed the Proclamation creating the new State. That was the year before I enlisted in the Union Army."

"Mr. Hall," said Mary Clifford, "when Father talks about when he was a boy, before the War, when there was slavery, it sounds just dreadful."

"What was it like when you were a boy, Mr. Hall?" Mary asked. "Did your family own slaves?"

"Mary Clifford," said J.R., "that is a very personal question! Please, Mr. Hall, excuse my daughter for prying into your family life!"

"Mr. Clifford," said Granville, "I don't mind that question at all. It is good for young people to understand our past."

"Miss Clifford," Granville continued, "our train is not due for a little while. If you will sit with me and my grandchildren, I will answer your question with a story from my childhood."

"That would be wonderful!—wouldn't it, Dad?" said Mary.

"Of course it would," said J.R.

Granville turned and spoke to his grandchildren. "Joshua and Deborah," he said, "this story is for you, too. It's about your great-grandparents—my mother, Mary Hall, and my father, John Hall."

"Do we have to?" asked Joshua. "We want to keep playing in the vines."

"Joshua," said Granville. "You will see, this is a an exciting story about young people just your age."

"OK," Joshua said, with slumped shoulders. "But it better be really exciting."

The group moved two station benches closer together, and Mary Clifford and her father sat down facing Granville and his grandchildren.

"This story happened in 1850, when I was thirteen years old," Granville began. "My sister Louisa and I were in our one-room schoolhouse in Shinnston, near Clarksburg."

CHAPTER TWO

Shinnston, Virginia, 1850

In the one-room schoolhouse in Shinnston, West Virginia, sunlight streamed through the tall windows, and shone on the polished wooden floors. A pot-bellied stove burned at the back of the room.

A dozen children of different ages and sizes sat at their desks. Their teacher, Miss Paxton, stood next to a large map hanging on the wall. It was a map of the State of Virginia.

"Granville Hall," Miss Paxton said, "please come up and point on the map to where we live."

Granville, a curly-haired boy of 13, stood up and walked to the front of the class. He bent forward for a few seconds to look closely at the map. Then he stood straight up and put his finger firmly down on the map, near its left edge.

"Shinnston is right here, Miss Paxton," said Granville, "just west of Clarksburg, in Harrison County, Virginia."

"Thank you, Granville," said Miss Paxton. Granville walked back to his seat.

"Now who wants to point to where the capitol of the State of Virginia is located?" asked Miss Paxton. "Seth, would you show us?"

Seth Goodman, a tall, red-haired boy, stood up and walked confidently to the front of the class. He quickly put his finger on another spot, this time almost on the map's opposite edge.

"The capitol of Virginia," Seth said, "is way over here—in Richmond."

A girl in the front row named Angela waved her hand. "Miss Paxton," she said, "why is the state capitol so far away from us? My mother says the people over in Richmond don't even know we exist!"

"Angela," said the teacher, "when they made Richmond the capitol of Virginia, there were hardly any people living here in the western part of the state. But today it's different."

In the back row, another girl raised her hand. She was Louisa Hall, Granville Hall's younger sister.

"Miss Paxton," said Louisa, "my father says we need to have our own state, so we can run our own affairs. He says the slave-owners are running the state for themselves."

"Louisa," said the teacher, "your father has a right to his opinion. But the law is the law, and right now, the laws are made in Richmond, and we must obey them."

Miss Paxton looked at the clock on the wall. She closed her lesson book. "It's time for recess," she said. "You may go outside while I put the next lesson on the board."

The children leapt up from their seats and hurried out of the classroom into the schoolyard.

Granville Hall was among the last to come outside. As he stepped out the door he was met by a chorus of chanting children, led by Seth Goodman.

"Granville is a 'blishonist! Granville is a 'blishonist!" Seth chanted, in a sing-song fashion.

The other children joined in: "Granville is a 'blishonist; Granville is a 'blishonist!"

"Granville's going to jail!" Seth said.

"Granville is a 'blishonist! Granville's going to jail," the other children chanted.

Louisa scowled. "Seth," Louisa said, balling up her fists, "you take that back, or I'm going to whip you."

Miss Paxton, holding an eraser and chalk in her hand, came out of the schoolhouse.

"Stop all this shouting," she said. "What's going on?"

"Miss Paxton," said Seth, "Granville is a 'blishonist, and his daddy is going to jail!"

Miss Paxton gave Seth an angry look. "Seth Goodman," she said, "you haven't the faintest idea what you are talking about." She glared at the other children. "You all go back inside to your seats," she said. "Granville and Louisa, please stay here. I see your parents coming down the street, and I think they need to speak with you."

Seth and the other children walked sheepishly past Miss Paxton and back into the schoolhouse.

Louisa and Granville saw their parents—Mary and John Hall—walking into the schoolyard. Their mother was wiping tears from her eyes. Louisa and Granville ran to their parents and embraced them.

"Mother! What's wrong?" cried Louisa. "Father! What are you doing here? Why aren't you at the tannery?"

John Hall, a serious-looking man with a dark brown beard, knelt down and put his arms around Louisa and Granville. "Children," said John, "your mother and I have something serious to discuss with you. I have to go away for a while."

"Are you going to jail, Father?" asked Granville. "Why did those kids call me a 'blishonist! I don't even know what that means!"

Mary put her hands on her son's shoulders. "Granville, those children are just ignorant," she said. "They are repeating something they heard. And the word they mean to say is 'abolitionist,'" she continued.

"An abolitionist is a person who wants to end all slavery. You know that your father and I believe that slavery is against God's will."

"You mean slavery... like when I saw those colored children chained together in Clarksburg?" asked Louisa.

"Yes, Louisa," Mary said. "Those children were taken from their mothers and bought and sold like cattle, and they are forced to work for nothing. If they try to run away from their owners, they are whipped like dogs—or even killed."

"It's even a crime to teach those enslaved children to read," said John. "We know that slavery is a sin against God and Man, and its days are numbered."

He gave his son a firm pat on the shoulder. "We abolitionists say 'end it now,' and the slave-owners say 'never.' Slavery is tearing our nation apart. Your mother and I hate slavery, and we pray every day for it to end."

"Why did Seth say you are going to jail, Father?" said Granville.

"Son, the Sheriff wants to arrest me and our neighbor because we have been reading anti-slavery newspapers," said John. "I'm going over to Ohio, while our friends try to get the charges dismissed. But I'm not frightened—and neither of you should be either."

"I'm not frightened; I'm mad!" said Louisa. "This is America, and we can read what we want!"

"Now Louisa and Granville, both of you need to be calm," Mary said. "God will protect your father."

John ruffled his children's hair.

"I must go now, and you need to finish your school day," he said, pointing back to the schoolhouse.

Miss Paxton, who had been watching from the school's doorway, took Granville and Louisa by the hand and led them back into the classroom. Both children fought back tears. Taking his wife's hand, John walked out of the schoolyard.

"What's going on, Granville?" asked the girl Angela, as Granville and Louisa took their seats.

"The Sheriff wants to put my father in jail because he's against slavery," said Granville.

"Your dad is a 'blishionist, too!" said Seth.

"Seth, you are as dumb as a fencepost," said Louisa. "An abolitionist *is* someone who is against slavery."

"Lots of people in our church are against slavery," said Angela. "And we don't even have any slaves in Shinnston."

"Well, there are rich people in Clarksburg who have slaves," said Seth. "I want to be rich and have slaves."

"That's because you don't like to do your own work, Seth!" said Louisa.

The other schoolchildren laughed at Louisa's remark. They knew Seth—and Louisa was right.

"I've seen slave children in Clarksburg, chained up to be sold," Louisa said, "and they are children just like us." She sat up straight at her desk. "Slavery is against God's will, and I'm against slavery in Virginia or anywhere else—and I can whip anyone who doesn't like it!"

"The Richmond government is the problem," Angela said. "That's what my father says."

"I don't know much about government," said Granville, "but I do know my folks are good Christians, and I want to be just like them when I grow up."

"If your father is so proud of his beliefs," Seth said, "then why is he running away?"

Granville looked at his sister, whose face was red and angry.

"You don't know what you're talking about, Seth," said Granville. "My dad said this is going to blow over, and I believe him."

"He's just scared!" said Seth.

Louisa jumped up, ran across the classroom, and pounced on Seth.

The red-headed boy fell backward onto the floor, with the furious girl on top of him, pummeling him with her clenched fists. Louisa landed several solid blows before Miss Paxton pulled Louisa off Seth, and dragged her back to her seat.

Then the fracas was over. In the silence, the schoolchildren could hear the "clip-clop" sound of the Sheriff's horse, passing by the schoolhouse and down the main street of Shinnston.

Under his breath, Granville said a prayer: "Oh, Father, be safe."

CHAPTER THREE

Parkersburg, West Virginia, 1913

Granville Hall, sitting on the train station bench, leaned back and sighed. Telling the story from his boyhood had brought back strong feelings.

"Okay, Grandpa. That was pretty exciting," said Joshua.

"What happened next?" Deborah asked. "I mean, what happened to your father, our great-grandpa?"

"My father was able to come home back from Ohio after a couple of months," said Granville. "The county finally dropped the charges. It was just political—the courthouse crowd was trying to look tough to please some of the wealthy slave-owners in our county."

"I never thought about white people getting into trouble for being against slavery," said Mary. "I guess 'abolitionist' was a dirty word when you were a boy."

"Miss Clifford, there were many whites like my parents who did not approve of slavery," said Granville, "but most of them were afraid to speak their true feelings."

J.R. Clifford had listened carefully to Granville Hall's story. Now he spoke.

"Mr. Hall," said J.R., "when I was a boy growing up near Moorefield, my father, Isaac Clifford, owned his own farm. We were free, but we couldn't vote. We couldn't travel without a pass, and we had no schools or teachers. My father could not read or write."

"I played with white children whose families lived nearby," J.R. continued. "Their parents were small farmers, and they didn't own any slaves. But there were also big farms and sawmills nearby, with many slaves. Sometimes those slaves escaped, and my family would help them."

"If I was a slave,' Joshua Hall said, "I would do anything to get free!"

"Good for you, Joshua," said J.R. with a smile. "You know, Mr. Hall, your story reminds me of a story from my own childhood."

"Please, Mr. Clifford—tell us," said Granville. "One good story deserves another!"

"Yes, please tell us," said Mary.

"Very well," said J. R. "It was in the summer of 1861, and I was still on the farm. My cousins and I had come in from working in the cornfield."

* * * * *

Williamsport, Virginia, 1861

Nestled in a valley among rolling hills was a white-washed one-story farmhouse, with a long covered porch along the front of the house.

The evening sun was just cresting the hill behind the house, sending long shadows from the trees around the house. J.R. Clifford and three other teenagers came across the farmhouse yard, and climbed up the front porch steps. They stacked their long-handled hoes by the door.

"Grandmother, where are you?" J.R. shouted. "We're done hoeing, and we're hungry!"

A white-haired woman with copper-colored skin came out of the house. She was carrying a basin filled with soapy, hot water. She put the basin on a table.

"Wash your hands, and wipe your boots—then you can go inside and eat," said Grandmother Clifford.

"Grandma," said J.R. as he washed his hands in the basin, "we heard a lot of horses going up and down the main road while we were hoeing corn. What's going on?"

"I don't know," said Grandmother Clifford, "but here comes your father. Maybe he knows."

Isaac Clifford came into the yard. He was tall, dark-skinned, and wearing overalls. Following just behind Isaac were a man and woman. The man had an iron bracelet and a short chain hanging from his wrist. The woman was shivering and clutched the man's arm.

"Father, are these people escaping to Pennsylvania?" J. R. asked.

"Hush, J. R.," Grandmother said sharply. "These people have no time for your questions."

"No problem, ma'am," said the young man with the iron bracelet. He spoke to J.R., while the other children listened and watched with wide eyes.

"Little brother," said the man, "we are headed for Pennsylvania. I want to join the Union Army. Our son was sold to a plantation down South—and if I have to shoot my way to Mississippi to bring him back, I will."

"But if that posse catches you," said Grandmother Clifford, "you're going to hang—and so will we!"

"Grandmother is right," said Isaac. "We need to go now."

"J.R.," Isaac said, "I am going to lead this couple to Cumberland, and I want you and your cousins to stay close to the farmhouse, and not attract attention."

"Yes, Father," J. R. said.

"Yes, sir," said the other children.

Isaac and the escaping slaves walked swiftly to the edge of the woods behind the farmhouse.

"Grandma, I want to fight for freedom, too," J. R. said.

"Take that, Johnny Reb!" shouted one of J.R.'s cousins. The other cousins began to dash around the porch, pretending to fire pistols.

"Hush!" said Grandmother Clifford. "Right now we have to be quiet and pray for Isaac."

"This war is just beginning, J.R.," Grandmother Clifford continued. "I'm afraid your time for fighting may come all too soon."

CHAPTER FOUR

Parkersburg, West Virginia, 1913

Mary Clifford took a handkerchief out of her pocket, and wiped her eyes. "Father," she said, "I am so proud of our Grandfather Isaac. Thank you for telling that story."

"I thank you, too," said Granville. "Your father was a brave man."

"Did your father get back home safely?" asked Joshua Hall.

"Yes, Joshua," J.R. replied. "My father knew the safe paths—and a few tricks, too. For one thing, he knew that old song, 'Wade in the Water.'"

"What do you mean?" asked Deborah Hall.

"Deborah," J.R. said, "'Wade in the Water' is a song that Harriet Tubman sang when she helped escaping slaves. The song taught them to stay in the river and creek beds where the slave-catchers' dogs would lose their scent."

"Wow! That's smart," Joshua said.

"Mr. Hall," said Mary, "after the Civil War began, how did you end up as a part of the Wheeling Convention?"

"Miss Clifford, when the war started," Granville said, "I was working for a newspaper called the *Wheeling Intelligencer*. They hired me to take down the speeches at the Statehood Convention in Wheeling."

"Not speeches," said Joshua, groaning. "I bet you were bored to death."

Granville smiled. "It was one of the most exciting times in

Independence Hall in Wheeling, 1861

my life." he said. "Wheeling was bustling and crowded. There were lots of factories, railroads, warehouses, and riverboats. The streets and wharves were crowded with wagons full of supplies, and the sidewalks were packed with people. Everyone came to Independence Hall, and people crowded inside to listen to the delegates debate about the new State."

"What did they say about slavery, Grandfather?" asked Deborah.

"All of the delegates wanted to stay in the United States, but many did not object to slavery," said Granville. "Others were like my parents, and were against slavery. Many thought that if we didn't end slavery, we would never get a new state admitted into the Union."

Granville closed his eyes for a moment, as if he was looking back in time. "I remember—I remember a great day in the Wheeling Convention when a great man, Captain Gordon Battelle, spoke against slavery."

"What did he say?" Joshua asked and then rolled his eyes. "I mean, now that you've told us everything else."

J.R. and Mary nodded their heads. "Yes, please tell us," they said.

*   *   *   *   *

Wheeling, Virginia, 1861

The third floor courtroom in Indepedence Hall was brightly lit by tall glass windows that were framed with ornate woodwork and stout cast-iron beams.

Inside the hall, the assembled Convention delegates were creating the new State of West Virginia.

At a desk in the delegates' area, a young man took his seat and laid out a pen, inkwell, and a pile of blank sheets of paper. It was Granville Hall, the Convention reporter.

The Convention chairman pounded his gavel to silence the hall. "The

Gordon Battelle

Chair holds that a quorum is present and calls this meeting to order," he said. "The Chair recognizes the Delegate from Ohio County, Gordon Battelle."

A dark-haired man wearing the uniform of a Union Army Captain, stood up and spoke firmly. "Mr. Chairman", he said, "I offer the following resolution: Resolved that on and after the fourth day of July, eighteen hundred and sixty-two, slavery or involuntary servitude, except for crime, shall cease within the limits of the new State of West Virginia."

Shouts of "Hear, hear!" came from the gallery.

"Order! Order!" the chairman said. "A resolution has been proposed. Is there discussion?"

A blonde-haired man in a dark suit stood up and raised his hand. The chairman said, "The Chair recognizes Delegate Raymond from Greenbrier County."

The blonde-haired man spoke loudly and with passion. "Mr. Chairman," he said, "the issue of slavery will divide this body. There are more than ten thousand Negro slaves in Western Virginia, and they represent great wealth to some of our leading citizens."

"How can we ask these men to support a new State, if it means they will lose their property? If nothing more is said about slavery here, I think all opposition to our new state will cease. I move to table Mr. Battelle's resolution, and I ask Mr. Battelle never to mention slavery here again."

Other voices in the gallery shouted, "Hear! Hear!"

"Order! Order!" the chairman repeated. "The Chair recognizes Delegate William Stevenson from Wood County."

Delegate Stevenson, a younger man, spoke more softly, but with great conviction. "Mr. Chairman," he said, "we have come here because we do not want to be a part of the Confederacy, which was formed to protect and perpetuate slavery. If we wish to be part of the United States, we must renounce slavery, even if some people must give up their slaves. I support the resolution."

The voices in the gallery were louder: "Bravo! Well said! Hear, hear! Hear, hear!"

The chairman said, "The Chair recognizes Delegate Battelle to close the debate."

The room was quiet, as Battelle looked around the room.

"Mr. Chairman," he said, "the injuries which slavery inflicts upon our own people are manifold and obvious. It practically aims to enslave not merely another race, but our own race."

Battelle continued, "It inserts in its bill of rights some very high sounding phrases securing the freedom of speech; and then puts a lock on every man's mouth and a seal on every man's lips who will not shout for and swear by the divinity of the slavery system."

"We want a new home for liberty!" someone yelled from the gallery.

At his table, young Granville Hall was writing down the passionate words that were being said. He felt a shiver of excitement.

"A day of reckoning is here—and justice is wielding her sword," he whispered to himself.

"A new home for liberty! A new home for liberty!" the crowd shouted.

CHAPTER FIVE

Parkersburg, West Virginia, 1913

"Mr. Hall," J.R. said, "thank you so much for telling us about Captain Battelle."

J.R. continued, "Am I correct that while the Captain exercised great eloquence, his opinion did not carry the day?"

"You do know your West Virginia history, Mr. Clifford, and you are correct," said Granville.

"Twenty-three delegates voted with Captain Battelle," said Granville, "but twenty-four voted to cut off any further discussion of slavery. So by just one vote, the Wheeling Convention sent Congress a Constitution that did not address the slavery issue. We feared that all our work would be for nothing."

"I believe Captain Battelle also paid the ultimate sacrifice, did he not?" J.R. asked.

"Yes, he did," said Granville. "The last time I saw Captain Battelle was at a Union Army camp near Alexandria."

"I visited Captain Battelle at the Army Hospital in Alexandria," said Granville. "He was ill when he left Wheeling, and we begged him not to go, but he insisted that his duty was there among his troops."

* * * * *

Alexandria, Virginia, 1862

There was just enough room for Granville Hall to pick his way among the dozens of wounded soldiers who were lying on the floor and cots of the medical tent.

"Excuse me," Granville said to a passing nurse. "I'm here to see Captain Gordon Battelle."

"Along the end, past the tent post," said the nurse. "I must warn you that he is not well."

Granville saw Gordon Battelle sitting in a wheelchair, wrapped in a ragged blanket. Battelle's skin was gray and glistening with sweat. As Granville approached, Battelle looked up, and spoke with surprise. "My dear young Granville Hall!" he said. "What are you doing here?"

"I've come to bring you the latest news, Captain," said Granville. "Congress has accepted our new state of West Virginia—but they insist that we include a slave emancipation clause in our constitution. The delegates in Wheeling are voting on that clause today. If they approve it, all we will need is the proclamation from President Lincoln!"

"That is good news," said Battelle—then he began coughing.

"Thank you," Battelle said. "Thank you for coming to tell me . . ." His coughing became violent and uncontrollable.

"Nurse, come quickly!" cried Granville.

The nurse brought Battelle a cup of water. She wiped the back of his neck and his forehead with a wet towel, and Battelle's coughing fit gradually eased.

He gestured to Granville to come close.

"Your news has brought me peace—and now, I'm ready to go home," Battelle said.

Then Gordon Battelle breathed a deep sigh. It was his last breath, and he closed his eyes forever.

At the tent's entrance, a soldier appeared. He approached Granville.

"This message just came for Captain Battelle," said the soldier to Granville, taking a folded paper from his pocket. "Can I give it to you?"

Granville took the telegram from the soldier and unfolded it. He wiped the tears from his eyes so he could see the text. He read the telegram's message aloud.

"Today the Wheeling Convention delegates voted overwhelmingly to add a slave emancipation clause to the new West Virginia Constitution, as required by Congress," he read.

Standing by Battelle's wheelchair, the nurse said, "Captain Battelle would have welcomed that news." "But why is the price of liberty always so high?" she continued. "Why must so much blood be shed?"

"I do not pretend to understand God's Providence," said Granville. "I only know that Captain Battelle has done his duty, and we must do ours. This war is far from over."

CHAPTER SIX

Parkersburg, West Virginia, 1913

Mary Clifford looked at Granville Hall, sitting across from her on the bench with his grandchildren.

"Mr. Hall," she said, "Captain Battelle was a great man, who gave his life to help make my people free. I will never forget this story."

"Captain Battelle was just one of many brave soldiers who died in his country's service," Granville said. "We owe them all a great debt."

"I wish I could've lived back then," said Joshua. "I'd have signed up to join the army right away."

"Mr. Clifford," Granville continued, "May I ask, if it is not too personal, how did you come to join the Union Army?"

"It was in the middle of the war," J.R. said. "There were Union forces camped near our farm, but there were also Rebel guerrillas all around us. My father was giving information to the Union troops, and he befriended a young Union officer from Chicago."

"You mean your father was a spy for the Union?" Joshua asked, his eyes wide.

"I guess he was, Joshua," J.R. said, nodding and smiling at the ever-curious boy.

"Father and Mother were afraid that the Rebels would try to harm our family," J.R. continued, "so with the help of this young officer they sent me to Chicago, where I stayed with his family and attended school."

"That's where I first learned to read," J.R. said. "There were black and white children in that school, and we were together in a classroom without regard to our skin color."

"I can read very well," said Deborah. "Can't I, Grandpa?"

"Yes, you can," said Granville, patting Deborah on her head. "And so can young Joshua here."

"Good for you," said J.R. "Reading is the key to understanding. And in my case, reading led me to joining the Army, a great adventure that changed my life."

"Tell us about it, Father," said Mary.

"Yes, do," said Granville.

"Very well," said J.R.

* * * * *

Chicago, Illinois, 1864

In a small apartment in the city of Chicago, young J.R. Clifford, in his shirtsleeves, was sitting at a small wooden kitchen table, talking with a short, older woman.

The woman, Mrs. Healy, stood at a sink; she was drying dishes while they talked. She wore a red-checkered apron over a pale blue seersucker housedress.

"Mrs. Healy," said J.R., "I need to talk to you about something important."

"What is it, J.R.?" Mrs. Healy said, wiping a glass with a dishtowel. "Are you having trouble with your homework?"

"No," J.R. said. "The homework is easy—I like the stories and poems that the teacher assigns. And the math is fun, too."

"Then what is on your mind?" Mrs. Healy asked.

J.R. took a folded piece of notebook paper out of his pocket.

"Last week I was looking at the newspaper that Mrs. Healy brings home," he said, "because now I can understand most of the words. And I read something in that paper that won't leave my mind."

Mrs. Healy put the dishtowel she was holding on the sink, and sat down at the table across from J.R. "What did the newspaper say?" she asked.

"I copied it out on this notebook paper," J.R. said, spreading the sheet out in front of him. "I must have read it a hundred times. It's part of a speech by Frederick Douglass, the escaped slave who is recruiting black soldiers for the Union Army."

"Frederick Douglass is a great man," said Mrs. Healy, the tips of her fingers reaching out to touch the edge of the creased paper. "Please read it to me. You know I read very poorly."

J.R. cleared his throat, and began to read: "Men of Color, to Arms! Who would be free themselves must strike the blow!"

"I urge you to fly to arms and smite to death the power that would bury the Government and your liberty in the same hopeless grave. This is your golden opportunity!'"

J.R. gave a quick, bright smile; then he continued: "Once let the black man get upon his person the brass letters 'U.S.', let him get an eagle on his button, and a musket on his shoulder and bullets in his pocket, and there is no power on earth that can deny that he has earned the right to citizenship.'"

J.R. looked up at the kind woman who had offered him care and shelter, far from his family. He said, "Mrs. Healy, I think Frederick Douglass is right."

Mrs. Healy's expression became serious.

"J.R. Clifford," she said, frowning, "your family sent you here so you would not be killed in this war. Do you think they would approve of your enlisting?"

"I know my family loves me," said J.R. "But now that I am sixteen, it is my decision. There are young men my age—black and white—who are fighting for our freedom. Last week two students from our school joined up."

J.R. reached across the table and laid his hand on top of hers. "Mrs. Healy," he said, "if the Union does not win, I may not have a home to return to."

Mrs. Healy looked closely at the young man across from her. He seemed different from the country boy whom she had taken in. He was becoming a young man—all too quickly.

"I saw the U.S. Colored Troops recruiter yesterday, and I enlisted!" J.R. said, speaking in an excited manner. "There is a train leaving for the training camp in Kentucky tomorrow, and I am to be on that train! I will write to my parents tonight, and I will mail my letter at the station."

U.S. Colored Troops

Mrs. Healy put her face in her hands. J.R. watched her, and waited. When she lifted her head, her cheeks and eyes glistened with tears.

"J.R. Clifford," she said," You are a brave and talented young man, and I am proud that you have learned so much in school. I guess I should not be surprised that you have used that learning to make a brave choice."

She reached across the table, and grasped J.R.'s hands in hers. "It has been a joy to have you in our home," she said. "I will pack a basket of food for your train trip. Mrs. Healy and I will pray every day that you will safely return home to your new state of West Virginia."

"Thank you, Mrs. Healy," J.R. said, squeezing her hands, "I don't know where this journey will lead, but I know I am doing the right thing."

CHAPTER SEVEN

Parkersburg, West Virginia, 1913

"Wow!" said Joshua. "Sixteen is not so old. Did they give you a gun?"

"Joshua," said J.R., "it's hard to believe, but not only did they give me a gun—because I could read, they made me a corporal, and I ended up commanding an artillery battery."

"Many of the soldiers were former slaves," J.R. continued. "They were uneducated but very brave. More than ten thousand colored soldiers died in the War. Just like Captain Battelle, we owe them a great debt."

For a moment they all sat silently, thinking of the victims and heroes of war. Then Granville Hall spoke.

"Mr. Clifford," he said, "thank you for your courage. When we celebrate our new State of West Virginia this week, it is indeed because of people like you and Captain Battelle."

Granville continued, "Mr. Clifford, I have one more question for you before our train leaves."

"How do you think that Negroes have fared in our new State?" he asked. "Did we succeed in creating a 'New Home for Liberty' for all West Virginians, whatever their color?"

J. R. thought for a second, and then replied in a serious tone.

"Mr. Hall, when I returned from the War," J.R. said, "I wanted to live in a state and a nation where the color of a person's skin was no more important than the color of their hair. But we have a long way to go to reach that goal."

J.R. continued, "Still, we have accomplished much in West Virginia that we can be proud of. We have tens of thousands of Negro voters. At a time when blacks are barred from voting throughout the South, we in West Virginia have even elected Negroes to our Legislature."

"And although our schools are segregated, we have many excellent teachers, and many of their best pupils are going to college—like my wonderful daughter Mary here, proud graduate of Storer College!"

"I wouldn't want to live in a state where people can't vote because of the color of their skin," said Deborah Hall. "That doesn't sound American to me!"

"Deborah," said Granville with a chuckle, "you sound a lot like your Great-Aunt Louisa."

Then Joshua spoke up.

"Grandpa," he said, "can you tell us what it was like at the Wheeling Convention, when West Virginia finally became a state?" Joshua asked.

"I suppose, Joshua," said Granville "—that I have time for one last story."

"Yes, yes!" said the others.

"It was after Congress approved the Statehood Bill." Granville said. "The word came from Washington that President Lincoln might veto the law. Everyone in Wheeling was on pins and needles."

* * * * *

Wheeling, Virginia, 1863

Newspaper reporters were crowded into the hallway of Independence Hall where Governor Francis Pierpont was answering questions. At the Governor's side, young Granville Hall took notes for the Convention record.

"Governor Pierpont, the city is buzzing with rumors," a reporter said. "Our readers want to know if President Lincoln will sign the Statehood Bill. What is your opinion?"

"Rather than give you an opinion," said Francis Pierpont, "I can read you the latest telegram that I sent President Lincoln."

Taking a copy of the telegram from his breast pocket, Pierpont read aloud in a clear, ringing voice:

"President Lincoln, I am in great hope you will sign the bill to make West Virginia a new state. The loyal troops from Virginia have their hearts set on it; the loyal people in the bounds of the new state have their hearts set on it; and if the bill fails, God only knows the result. I fear general demoralization, and I must not be held responsible."

"Will the President act soon?" asked a reporter.

Pierpont spoke, again with strong emotion: "I do not know what the President will do," he said, "but we have laid the case before him as strongly as we can. The President knows that we love the Union. I believe he will hear our cry."

* * * * *

Washington, DC, 1863

Three hundred miles to the East, President Abraham Lincoln took up a pen and put his thoughts to paper.

"We can scarcely dispense with the aid of West Virginia in this struggle," Lincoln wrote, "much less can we afford to have her against us in Congress and in the field. Her brave and good men regard her admission into the Union as a matter of life and death."

"West Virginia has made the changes in her Constitution required by Congress providing for the abolition of slavery in the new state."

"Therefore, pursuant to the authority granted to me by the Congress of the United States, I hereby proclaim that on June 20, 1863 and for all time thereafter, there will be a new star in Old Glory—a new home for liberty in the United States—the State of West Virginia!"

*   *   *   *   *

Parkerburg, West Virginia, 1913

"When Lincoln signed the statehood proclamation, there was great rejoicing in Wheeling," said Granville. "Of course, it was bittersweet, because so many good people who had fought for statehood had died in the war, and were not there to see the fruits of their labors. But they were present in our hearts."

"Dad, Mr. Hall," said Mary Clifford, "thank you for telling us these wonderful stories."

"Yes, thank you!" said Joshua and Deborah.

The train whistle blew, and dark smoke billowed from the engine's stack. Granville Hall and his grandchildren stood up from the railroad station bench. J. R. Clifford and Mary Clifford rose as well. They all shook hands and parted.

These historic characters had shared a magical moment.

Thank you, reader, for sharing it with them.

God bless the State of West Virginia—our "New Home for Liberty."

"J. R. CLIFFORD AND THE CARRIE WILLIAMS CASE"
BY THOMAS RODD

CHAPTER ONE

Martinsburg, West Virginia, 1913

It was a warm, windy, fall day in Martinsburg, West Virginia, in the year 1933.

Fluffy white clouds raced across the blue sky. Red and gold leaves swirled through the streets, painting the sidewalks and porches with bright colors.

In the parlor of a large white house in Martinsburg's "colored" section, a tall older man with dark skin and a full head of white hair stood at a wooden desk. He wore a white shirt and dark pants and held a wooden cane loosely in one hand.

The man was John Robert Clifford, Esq., a lawyer. He was known to his friends and colleagues as "J.R." and to his extended family as "Uncle John." He was eighty-three years old.

In a church across the street, a gospel choir was rehearsing. J.R. could hear the singers' voices rise and fall over the rhythmic chords of a piano.

For a moment J.R. stood still and listened to the music, tapping his foot softly on the carpet. Then he returned his attention to the desk, and picked up several dozen sheets of yellowing paper. They were the typed transcript of a court hearing.

"I knew I had kept this transcript," J.R. said to himself with pleasure. He read the first page, which began with a question: "Please state your name and occupation."

The next line read: "My name is Carrie Williams. I am a schoolteacher at the colored school in the Town of Coketon, Fairfax District, in Tucker County, West Virginia."

J.R. stopped reading. Steadying himself with the cane, he crossed the parlor and lowered himself into an upholstered chair. He laid the transcript in his lap, leaned back, and closed his eyes.

Carrie Williams

A soprano soloist was singing now in the church, calling out her praise to God, each time answered by the choir. J.R.'s thoughts floated freely with the music.

Suddenly, his rest was interrupted by the noisy arrival of J.R.'s great-niece, Freda Clifford.

Freda, a lively nine-year-old girl in a white sundress, ran into the parlor and grabbed J.R.'s arm, shaking him awake.

"Uncle John," Freda said loudly, "stop snoozing! I have an important message for you from Aunt Mary!"

J.R. opened his eyes. He smiled indulgently at the excited girl. "What is it, Freda?" J.R. asked.

"Uncle John, Mrs. Carrie Williams just called over to Aunt Mary's," said Freda. "Mrs. Williams said she would arrive here in half an hour." Freda cocked her head to one side. "Who is Mrs. Williams, Uncle John?" she asked.

"Freda, Mrs. Williams is a former client of mine," said J.R. "She wrote and said she might visit me today. Mrs. Williams was the plaintiff in an important case, one that happened a long time ago—before you were even born."

Freda, sensing a good story, rose up on her toes, and hung her head and arms over the back of J.R.'s chair. She patted her great-uncle's thick white hair with her hands.

"Was it a fun case, Uncle John?" Freda asked. "Did the good guys win?"

J.R. shook his head and laughed. "Not exactly fun, Freda," he said, "—but very important." He held up the papers in his lap. "In fact, I have the transcript of Mrs. Williams' trial right here."

"Wow! Will you read it to me?" asked Freda. "Please?"

"Perhaps–we'll see when Mrs. Williams gets here."

"Thank you, Uncle John. I can't wait! I better make us some lemonade," and she dropped off the chair and ran into J.R.'s kitchen.

The choir in the church next door began to sing "Nearer, My God to Thee." J.R. leaned back in his chair and closed his eyes. He remembered the day that he first met Carrie Williams.

CHAPTER TWO

The Town of Coketon, West Virginia, is located in Tucker County, in the northern highlands of the Mountain State, at the head of the Blackwater River Canyon.

Historic Marker, Coketon, West Virginia

Today Coketon has only a few residents, but in the 1890s Coketon was the bustling headquarters of the biggest railroad, timber, and coal enterprise in West Virginia—the Davis Coal and Coke Company, owned by the industrialist Henry Gassaway Davis.

Beginning in the 1880s, thousands of men, women, and children moved to the Coketon area. They came to mine coal, to make "coke" from coal for the steel industry, to work on the railroad, and to cut trees and saw lumber.

Hundreds of these newcomers were called "Negro," "colored," or "black"—because they had African ancestry. Like other immigrants to Tucker County, these African American citizens wanted their children to receive a good education. Following West Virginia law of the time, which mandated segregated schools, the Tucker County Board of Education set up a one-room "colored school" in Coketon.

* * * * *

Coketon, West Virginia, 1892

On a cool morning in October of 1892, J.R. Clifford stepped down from a railroad passenger car onto the train station platform in Coketon. J.R. wore a brown three-piece suit, a starched white shirt, and shiny brown leather boots. He carried a leather briefcase in one hand, and in his other hand he held a brass-tipped walking stick.

The streets of Coketon were noisy and dusty, full of wagons and carts that were pulled by horses and mules. Men and women hurried in and out of stores and warehouses. A few tall trees stood along the rim of the Blackwater Canyon, high above the town, lonely survivors of the wave of construction that had recently built this "boom town" in the West Virginia wilderness.

J.R. began to walk south toward the brick Buxton and Landstreet company store building. His boots clacked on the wooden sidewalk.

The sidewalk ended just beyond the company store. J.R.

continued on a well-worn gravel path, past a long row of smoking brick-clad ovens that towered over his head. The ovens cooked the raw coal into coke to be used in making steel. A crew of dark-skinned, muscled workmen, shoveling coke into a railroad car, paused a moment from their exertions and gave J.R. a respectful nod as he passed. He returned a salute to the workmen, and continued walking.

As J.R. reached the outskirts of town, he saw a rough-sawn wooden school building, just a few yards from the banks of the Blackwater River. Several children were outside the school, playing on the rocks beside the river. The children saw J.R. approaching and ran into the building.

"He's here, Mrs. Williams!" said a boy as he took his seat in the schoolroom.

The wooden floor of the schoolroom shone with polishing. Late wildflowers and milkweed pods were placed in vases on each windowsill. A coal-burning stove gave off a warm glow.

Schoolteacher Carrie Williams, a slender young woman, stood in front of her class. Two rows of girls, with tidy bows in their hair, and two rows of boys, with their clean shirts buttoned all the way to the top, were seated on benches. The children ranged in age from eight to sixteen.

"Students," said Carrie to her pupils, "today we are going to have a special visitor—Mr. John Robert Clifford, from Martinsburg, West Virginia. Mr. Clifford is a distinguished lawyer and newspaper publisher."

"Mr. Clifford is visiting our school on behalf of Storer College in Harpers Ferry, West Virginia, where they are training schoolteachers for our colored schools," Carrie continued. "He will make a report to the College, so I want you to be on your best

Original building, Storer College

behavior." Carrie straightened her blue dress, and patted her braids in place.

The schoolroom door opened, and J.R. Clifford stepped inside and closed the door behind him. He crossed the room to greet Carrie.

"Good morning," J.R. said, shaking Carrie's hand. "I am J.R. Clifford. It is a pleasure to visit your school, Teacher Williams."

"Good morning to you, Mr. Clifford," replied Carrie. "We are honored that you came to visit us. Let me introduce you to my pupils." Carrie motioned to the children to stand. "Class," she said, "this is Mr. J.R. Clifford."

The children stood, and said in unison, "Good morning, Mr. Clifford."

"Good morning, students," said J.R. "I am so glad to see you all attending school this morning. Many brave people gave their lives in the Civil War so that you would have the right to an education."

The children sat down. J.R. stood at the front of the room, and planted the tip of his stick between his feet on the polished floor. "Please, children," he said, "feel free to ask me any questions you like."

Marcus, a tall boy in the front row, stuck up his hand.

"Mr. Clifford, were you . . .?" Marcus began, and then his voice broke upward, causing the other children to giggle.

Carrie Williams gave her students a stern look. "Continue, Marcus," she said.

"Mr. Clifford," asked Marcus, "were you a soldier in the Civil War?"

"Yes, Marcus," J.R. replied. "When I was sixteen years old, I enlisted in the Union Army. I served in the United States Colored Troops, in the 13th Heavy Artillery."

Whispers rose from the children. A soldier!

"But I hated war and killing people," J.R. said, "so today I fight for justice using the law, the vote, and the power of the press. I am publishing a newspaper, the Pioneer Press, that reports the accomplishments and concerns of people of color."

The Pioneer Press

Kimberly, a younger girl with big, serious eyes, raised her hand. "Did you know John Brown, Mr. Clifford?" Kimberly asked.

"No," said J.R. "When John Brown and his raiders attacked the arsenal at Harpers Ferry in 1859, I was only eleven years old. But I remember my father and grandfather talking about the courage of Brown and his men—black and white—who took up arms to abolish slavery in this Nation."

"I'm eleven right now," said Kimberly, with a shy smile.

"Then, young lady," said J.R., "maybe this year the world has great things in store for you, too!"

Kimberly blushed.

"Children," Carrie Williams said, "did you know that Mr. Clifford grew up not far from here?"

"That's right, Mrs. Williams," said J.R. "Before the Civil War, my family lived on a farm in Williamsport, near Moorefield, just over the mountain."

"Although there were many, many slaves in Virginia, my parents and grandparents were free blacks, and we owned our own farm. I loved our country life, but in Virginia, there were no schools for colored people, so my family sent me to Chicago to get an education."

J.R. looked at the children's bright, attentive faces. He leaned forward and spoke intently.

"I missed my family and friends," said J.R., "but the education I got was invaluable. There were children of all backgrounds and races in my school. Education is so important for your future. Don't ever forget that!"

"It was in Chicago that I enlisted in the Army," J.R. continued. "Then, when the War was over, I continued my education at Storer College, and became a schoolteacher and principal in Martinsburg. After that, I started my newspaper. And five years ago, in 1887, I passed the bar examination and became West Virginia's first African American attorney. I hope that one or two of you children may follow in my shoes. We need more black lawyers in this young state!"

J.R. turned to Carrie Williams. "Mrs. Williams, your children ask wonderful questions. May I ask them some questions of my own?"

"Certainly," said Carrie. "I hope they will give good answers!"

J.R. pointed to his young audience. "Now, children, you tell me—what are your plans and dreams?"

Marcus was the first to raise his hand.

"Mr. Clifford," he said, "my dream is to be an engineer. My father is working on the railroad in the Blackwater Canyon; building stone bridges over the waterfalls. I want to learn to build those big bridges."

J.R. nodded his head with approval. "Very good, Marcus," he said.

In the back row, Walter, a small boy with a wide smile, hopped up from his seat.

"Mr. Clifford," Walter said, "my dream is to be a musician. I love the music of all the different people in Coketon—the Italians, the Croatians, and the colored people. I want to play in an orchestra and play the music of the whole world!"

"That is a worthy goal, young man," said J.R. "The world needs artists as well as engineers."

A dark girl with glasses and her hair in a bun shyly held up her hand.

"Go ahead, Mary, tell us your dreams," said Carrie Williams.

Mary stood and folded her hands in front of her. "Mr. Clifford," she said softly, "I love our school in Coketon, and I love our beautiful river valley. My dream is to be a teacher like Mrs. Williams. But I am afraid that there won't be any teaching jobs for me. My father says that the School Board is cutting the term of our school."

"Young lady, you must follow your dream to be a teacher," said J.R. "And I encourage all of you to follow your dreams. If you work hard, you can succeed—no matter what the obstacles!"

"Now, children," said Carrie, "get out your books and continue with your lessons, while I talk to Mr. Clifford privately, and thank him for joining us today."

The two adults walked to the end of the schoolroom, opened the door, and stepped out onto the porch. The river rippled over the rocks with a soft burbling noise, and the pungent smell of smoke from the coke ovens was strong.

"Mrs. Williams," said J.R., "I am most disturbed to hear that the School Board is cutting your school term. Can you tell me more about this?"

"What Mary said is true," said Carrie. "The School Board has refused to pay for a full eight months for our school in Coketon. The white children will have eight months, but our colored school term will only be five months."

"Will no one challenge the School Board?" asked J.R.

"No," said Carrie. "The School Board is run by the Davis Coal and Coke Company. If the children's parents protest, they will lose their jobs. But I refused to sign a five-month contract," she said, shaking her head. "I knew it was wrong."

J.R. looked down for a moment; then he raised his head.

"I have an idea, Mrs. Williams," he said. "Could you continue teaching after five months have passed, if the School Board stops paying you? Do you have any savings that you could live on?"

"Yes, I could," said Carrie. "My husband, Abraham, and I have been saving for several years, and we have a nest egg that we could use."

"Good," said J.R. "Let me consult my law books when I get back to Martinsburg, and I will write to you. But I am telling you now—do not plan to stop teaching after five months. There will be a financial risk to you, but we may be able to beat the School Board at their own game!"

"I love teaching, and I love these children, Mr. Clifford," Carrie replied. "Continuing to teach will not be hard."

The steam whistle blew from the railroad engine at the train station. J. R. took a watch from his vest pocket. "I must be going," he said. "The train leaves for Martinsburg in ten minutes."

J.R. opened the school door and stepped inside with Mrs. Williams. The children stopped talking and looked at J.R. expectantly.

"Children, thank you for having me in your school today," he said. "I am very proud of all of you. But now I must leave. You do as

Mrs. Williams tells you, and make your parents proud of you."

"Goodbye, Mr. Clifford," the children said. They waved goodbye to their distinguished visitor. The lawyer gave the children a salute in reply, and walked out of the school.

Carrie Williams stayed in the schoolroom and closed the door. "Children," she said, "thank you for being so good while Mr. Clifford visited us."

Mary raised her hand. "Teacher Williams, can we sing a song before lunch?" she asked.

"Mary, that's a wonderful idea," said Carrie. "What song would you like to sing?"

"What about the song that they sang in the Civil War, when Mr. Clifford was fighting for our freedom?" said Mary. "You know—'Glory, Glory, Hallelujah!'"

"That's a very good choice, Mary," said Carrie. She motioned to the children to stand, and led the students in singing "The Battle Hymn of the Republic."

As J.R. walked away from the school, he heard the children's high, clear voices. He remembered how he and his fellow soldiers had sung that song marching into battle. He remembered the rough woolen coat scratching his neck and the weight of the rifle against his shoulder. He remembered the smell of gunpowder, and the cries of men at war.

The train whistle blew a second time, and J. R. picked up his pace. As he walked toward the station, he hummed the tune that the children were singing—"His truth is marching on!"

A strategy for Carrie Williams' case was brewing in his mind.

CHAPTER THREE

Martinsburg, West Virginia, 1913

Standing in J.R.'s parlor in Martinsburg, young Freda Clifford shook her great-uncle's arm.

"Uncle John," said Freda, "Wake up! Mrs. Williams is here!"

J. R. opened his eyes just as Carrie Williams—now a handsome woman in her sixties, with gray hair and a wreath of wrinkles around her bright eyes—walked into the parlor.

Carrie wore a blue woolen traveling suit. She crossed the room and took J.R.'s hands in hers. "My dear old friend!" she said as she sat down in a chair across from J.R.

J.R.'s face beamed with pleasure. "Mrs. Williams, how long has it been? I guess more than thirty years!" he said. He took Carrie Williams' hands, and gave them a firm squeeze.

"Tell me," he said, "what brings you to our humble Martinsburg? The last I heard, you had moved to Chicago."

"You are correct, Mr. Clifford," said Carrie. "But my youngest daughter is now a teacher at the Sumner School in Martinsburg, and I have come to visit her."

"Sumner School! Why, that's my old school!" J.R. exclaimed. "I started teaching there in 1877, nearly fifty years ago—how time flies!"

Freda, who had gone into the kitchen, came back into the parlor carrying a tray with three glasses on it.

"Here's some lemonade, Mrs. Williams," Freda said. "Fresh squeezed!"

"Thank you, sweet girl," said Carrie, taking a glass. She sipped the cool drink and looked closely at J.R. "You seem very well, Mr. Clifford," Carrie said. "Are you still practicing law?"

"Yes, Mrs. Williams, I am," J.R. replied, "as much as my eighty-five-year-old body will let me!"

Freda pulled up a stool beside her uncle's chair and sat on it. "Uncle John," Freda said, "why don't you show Mrs. Williams your famous shirt?"

"What shirt is that, Mr. Clifford?" Carrie asked politely.

J.R. pointed to the far wall. "Over there," he said. "I was wearing that shirt in a Martinsburg courtroom in 1895, when the prosecuting attorney attacked me."

Carrie looked across the room. A man's white dress shirt, covered with dark brown patches, hung on a hook on the wall.

Carrie frowned with concern. "Why did the prosecutor attack you?"

"I insisted on having black citizens on the jury," J.R. answered. "When the prosecutor struck me with a paperweight, the blood ran from my head into my shoes, and stained my shirt forever. But they are stains of courage, and so I display them proudly."

"But you beat him, Uncle John!" said Freda. "You socked it to him, right?"

Carrie and J.R. laughed at Freda's enthusiasm.

"Yes, Freda, I beat him," said J.R. "I campaigned all over the county against his election, and I waved that bloody shirt!" He smiled at the recollection. "That scoundrel lost by 1,300 votes. That was a productive year, 1898—the same year that we finally won your case, Mrs. Williams."

"I often think about our case," said Carrie.

"I do as well," said J.R. "In fact," he continued, "I have the transcript of the trial right here." J. R. showed Carrie the papers that were lying in his lap. "Freda wants me to tell her the story."

Freda clapped her hands. "Yes, Uncle John, please tell me all about it!"

"Please do, Mr. Clifford," said Carrie Williams. She smiled and sipped her drink.

"Very well," J.R. said, as he picked up the transcript from his lap. "The trial took place in 1895. It had taken two years to get our case before a jury. But it was worth the wait!"

CHAPTER FOUR

Parsons, West Virginia, 1895

The year was 1895. In the front of the Tucker County courtroom in Parsons, West Virginia, attorney J.R. Clifford and his client Carrie Williams sat quietly at a wooden table. Carrie wore her blue Sunday dress; J. R. Clifford wore a spotless gray suit.

Historic Marker, Parsons, West Virginia

At another table, about ten feet away, two white lawyers sat and whispered to each other. Several dozen Tucker County residents, a mixture of better-dressed townspeople and workers in coarser clothing, sat behind a railing in the courtroom's audience section.

Carrie turned in her seat to look at her husband Abraham, who was sitting in the front row of the audience. Abraham, a handsome, wiry man, gave Carrie a reassuring grin and a wink that made her relax a little.

Carried smiled back at Abraham, and then she faced forward. She spoke to J. R., who was scratching last-minute notes with a fountain pen.

"Did you enjoy your trip through the Blackwater Canyon, Mr. Clifford?" Carrie asked.

"I did, Mrs. Williams," said J.R. "I believe that is the steepest railroad grade I have ever ridden on. But those powerful engines and wonderful stone bridges make for a comfortable ride. Abraham should be proud of his work on the track crew."

"He is," said Carrie. "And I am glad he could get off work today for our trial. I am so worried."

"All we can do is tell the truth and ask for justice," said J.R. "The rest is out of our hands."

A door at the side of the courtroom opened. The bailiff, who took his place beside the judge's bench, wore a silver badge on his dark uniform shirt. A court reporter wearing a string tie sat at a small desk in front of the judge's bench, ready to take notes for the transcript.

Carrie turned and looked nervously one more time at Abraham; he gave Carrie another reassuring nod.

"Oyez, oyez, oyez!" the bailiff called out loudly. "The Circuit Court of Tucker County is now in session, the Honorable Joseph T. Hoke presiding."

Circuit Judge Hoke, an older man in a long black robe with

Judge Hoke

a sober expression on his face, came into the courtroom and took his seat behind the bench.

"Good morning, everyone," said Judge Hoke, with a nod to the lawyers.

"I have one preliminary matter that I need to take care of," said the Judge. "As you may know, I was associated with Storer College as a Trustee for many years, and Mr. Clifford is a graduate of Storer. Does either party think I need to step aside in this case?"

J.R. stood up at his table and replied to the Judge's question. "I certainly do not have a problem with this fact, your Honor."

At the facing table sat the lawyer for the School Board, C.O. Streiby—a tall man with piercing eyes. Beside Streiby sat School Board Secretary Harold Meyer. Meyer wore an expensive-looking coat and sported a handlebar moustache.

Streiby consulted with Meyer for a moment; then he rose to his feet. "We have no objection to your Honor presiding," said Streiby.

"Very well," said Judge Hoke. "Let's get right to this morning's case. Mr. Bailiff, please summon the jury."

The bailiff opened the jury room door. Twelve men of varying ages filed into the courtroom and took their seats in the jury box. Some had olive-tinged skin, characteristic of the many Italians who had come to work in Tucker County's mines and sawmills.

Judge Hoke turned in his chair to face the jurors and cleared his throat.

"Members of the jury," the Judge said, "today we have a case in which the plaintiff, Mrs. Carrie Williams, a schoolteacher in Coketon, has sued the Tucker County Board of Education for three months' salary."

"Mrs. Williams' attorney is Mr. J.R. Clifford of Martinsburg," Judge Hoke continued. He turned to the table where Carrie and J.R. sat. "Mr. Clifford," said the judge, "call your first witness."

"We call the plaintiff, Carrie Williams," said J.R.

Carrie Williams stood up and walked without hesitation to the witness stand. In one hand, she carried a brown folder.

Carrie nodded to the judge and jury and sat down. The bailiff asked Carrie if she swore to tell the truth, so help her God.

"I do," she said with conviction.

J.R. walked closer to the witness stand.

"State your name and occupation," said J.R. Clifford. His strong voice carried to the back of the courtroom.

"My name is Mrs. Carrie Williams," Carrie replied, pronouncing her words precisely, just as if she were in her classroom. "I am a schoolteacher at the colored school in the Town of Coketon, Tucker County, West Virginia."

"Mrs. Williams," J.R. asked, "In the 1892 and 1893 school year, did you have a written teaching contract with the School Board?"

"No," said Carrie. "The School Board refused to give me a contract for eight months like the contracts they gave the white schoolteachers. The Board wanted me to sign a contract for only five months. But I would not sign it."

"Mrs. Williams," asked J.R., "what happened after five months?"

'I kept on teaching," Carrie said. "But the School Board would not continue to pay me."

Carrie looked for a moment at Abraham in the courtroom audience—then she spoke directly to the jury. "My husband and I used our savings to live, so I could give my pupils a fair and legal education," she said. "I am still owed three months' wages—one hundred and twenty dollars."

"So it was solely a desire for a fair education for your students that motivated you?" J.R. asked.

"Fair—and legal," Carrie said forcefully.

J.R. turned to the Judge. "Your Honor," J.R. said, "I have no further questions. Mr. Streiby may inquire."

J. R. sat down, and the School Board's lawyer C. O. Streiby rose from his seat to approach the witness stand.

Streiby directed a hard gaze at Carrie. "Mrs. Williams," said Streiby, "at the end of the five months, didn't School Board Secretary Meyer tell you that he would not give you any more payments? And didn't he also demand that you give him the class register?"

Carrie squared her shoulders. "Yes, he did," she replied.

Streiby's voice dripped with accusation. "But you did not give Mr. Meyer the class register that he requested, did you?" he asked.

"No, I kept it," said Carrie, "and I kept on teaching for the full eight months." She opened the folder in her hand and held up a dark blue book. "Here is the completed register."

Streiby reached out his hand to take the register from Carrie. But instead of giving the book to Streiby, Carrie opened it and began to read from its contents. Streiby slowly withdrew his hand, a look of surprise on his face.

"The register shows that I taught for a full eight months," Carrie said. "We covered eight subjects: orthography, reading, penmanship, arithmetic, grammar, history, geography, and language lessons."

She continued, "They are good children. They all worked hard at their studies, and . . ."

"Excuse me, Teacher Williams," interrupted Streiby, his voice rising. "The only reason," he said, "— the only reason that you give for teaching eight months—is because the white children had eight months, and not because you had a contract?"

"Yes," said Carrie coolly. "That is correct."

"And," she added, looking again at the jurors, "I believe it is the law."

Streiby shook his head, as if to marvel at Carrie's audacity in defying the School Board.

"No further questions, your Honor," Streiby said. He walked back to his table and sat down next to Harold Meyer, who was also shaking his head in incredulity.

"Mr. Clifford," asked Judge Hoke, "do you have any re-direct examination?"

"I have no further questions, your Honor," said J.R. "However, I do ask that the class register be admitted into evidence and shown to the jury."

"Your Honor," said Streiby, rising up from his chair in protest, "we see no relevance to the class register. They are just standard notes, after all."

"You brought up the subject of the register," Judge Hoke said firmly. "I will admit it into evidence, and the jury may take it into account in their deliberations."

Judge Hoke continued. "Mrs. Williams, you may take your seat. Mr. Clifford, call your next witness."

"Your Honor," said J.R, "we call Mr. Harold A. Meyer."

Harold Meyer gave a little jerk when he heard his name; he did not expect that J.R. call him as a witness. Meyer and Streiby whispered to each other briefly, and then Meyer stood up stiffly, walked to the witness chair, and was sworn in by the bailiff.

"State your name and occupation," said J.R. to Meyer.

"My name is Harold A. Meyer," Meyer said. His tone was nervous and hesitant. "I am the vice-president of the Davis Coal and Coke Company, and . . . and . . . uh—I am also the Secretary of the School Board of Tucker County."

"Mr. Meyer," asked J.R., "the School Board sets the property taxes for the District, and those taxes pay for all of the schools in the District, white and colored—isn't that correct?"

"That's correct," Meyer replied, visibly relieved to be asked a simple question.

"In the 1892-1893 school year, Mr. Meyer," continued J.R., "the colored children's school received funds for five months, while the white children's school received funds for eight months. Why was that, Mr. Meyer?" J.R. asked. His calm tone suggested an innocent curiosity.

"Well, Mr. Clifford," Meyer replied, now with more confidence in his voice, "it was simple arithmetic. We calculated the number of white children in the district and the number of colored children. There were less colored, so their share of the taxes only allowed for five months of school."

"Let me ask you this, Mr. Meyer," J.R. asked, in a more pointed tone. "Could you not raise the property taxes, so as to pay for a full eight-month term of school for both white and colored children?"

Harold Meyer's eyes darted about the courtroom. Flustered by the unexpected question, he took a handkerchief from his pocket and patted his head.

"Why. . . .," Meyer stammered, "why, . . . to do that would cost more for each colored pupil than for each white pupil, because there are less of the colored. I mean, that would be entirely irregular, and . . .."

"Objection!" C.O. Streiby said hotly, rising out of his chair. "The question calls for speculation!"

Judge Hoke nodded his head and said calmly, "The objection is sustained."

J.R. showed no reaction to the judge's ruling. Streiby nodded his head with satisfaction and sat down.

J.R. continued his questioning.

"Mr. Meyer," he asked, "does the Davis Coal and Coke Company own large tracts of property in Tucker County, and pay most of the school property tax?"

"Your Honor!" said Streiby, rising to his feet again, "I fail to see the relevance of this question."

"Your Honor," said J. R, "as the Court must appreciate, the question goes to the witness' motive."

"I agree, Mr. Clifford," said Judge Hoke. "The objection is overruled."

Streiby shook his head and sat down.

"What is your answer, Mr. Meyer?" asked J.R. "Doesn't your company have a direct interest in keeping the school taxes as low as possible?"

"Well... umm, well," Harold Meyer stuttered, said, "of course, the Davis Coal and Coke Company... uh... does pay a large portion of the property tax—but that's not... I mean to say..."

"Thank you, Mr. Meyer. I have no further questions," J.R. stated and sat down.

Judge Hoke turned to Streiby. "Mr. Streiby, any cross-examination?"

Harold Meyer looked anxiously at Streiby.

"Yes, indeed, your Honor!" said Streiby vigorously, as he rose and approached his client.

"Mr. Meyer," asked Streiby, "is your service on the Board of Education solely a public service to the community?"

Harold Meyer straightened his shoulders and looked confidently at the jury. "Yes, sir!" Meyer replied. "And on behalf of Davis Coal and Coke, I can tell you that our company has a strong interest in maintaining an educated and contented work force."

"Of course you do!" said Streiby. "And, Mr. Meyer, were you at all times acting within the law as you understood it?"

The corners of J.R.'s mouth lifted in a slight smile. He stood and addressed the Judge.

"Objection, your Honor," said J.R. "It is irrelevant what this witness thought the law was."

"I agree," said the Judge. "The objection is sustained."

Harold Meyer's face turned red.

Streiby gave a frustrated sigh. "Your Honor, I have no further questions," he said and sat down.

Judge Hoke turned to J.R. "Mr. Clifford, do you have any redirect examination of this witness?"

"No, your Honor," said J.R. "The plaintiff Mrs. Carrie Williams rests her case. We believe our evidence is sufficient to show that Mrs. Carrie Williams should be paid $120.00 for her teaching services."

C.O. Streiby, seeing that nothing would be gained by submitting further evidence, stood and addressed the Judge.

"Your Honor," said Streiby, "the Defendant also rests. We believe our evidence is sufficient to show that Mrs. Williams had no contract and is not owed any sum."

"Very well. You may take your seat, Mr. Meyer," said Judge Hoke.

Harold Meyer stepped down from the witness box and joined Streiby at their table.

Judge Hoke stroked his chin and looked down at the court papers on his desk. After a moment, the Judge lifted his head and turned to speak to the men in the jury box.

"Members of the jury," said Judge Hoke, "it is now my task to instruct you in the law. Then the attorneys will make their arguments, and it will be your task to deliberate and render a verdict."

Judge Hoke read from the notes on his desk, speaking slowly and deliberately. "The court instructs you that the Constitution of the State of West Virginia provides that whites and colored shall not be educated in the same school. The law also requires the Board of Education to establish schools for the equivalent education of the colored children in the District."

Judge Hoke looked intently at the twelve men in the jury box. "The court instructs you," said the Judge, "that a person may not seek payment for a task without a contract. But it is also true that every contract must comply with the law."

"Your verdict," said the Judge, "must be based upon these fundamental legal rules that I have presented to you."

"Mr. Clifford," Judge Hoke said, "you may address the jury."

J.R. stood and faced the twelve men in the jury box. J.R. was the first African American lawyer whom any of the jurors had encountered, and they gave him their close attention.

"Thank you all," said J.R., "for your attention to teacher Carrie Williams' case."

"The simple issue that you must decide," he said, "is whether the School Board must follow the law of the State of West Virginia. That law requires that the Board must provide the necessary funds for the colored children's schooling,—even if it means that the Davis Coal and Coke Company will pay more in taxes."

J.R. gestured toward Carrie Williams. "My client, Mrs. Carrie Williams, followed the law. It is the School Board that deviated from the law."

"Mrs. Carrie Williams earned her pay, teaching every school day for three months," said J.R., "She is a hard-working and law-abiding citizen of this nation. And yes, I see such citizens before me at this moment."

The jurors—reminded by J.R. that they, too, worked for a living—had thoughtful looks on their faces.

"No matter what the color of a person's skin is," J.R. continued, "here in America, all workers deserve full and fair pay for the work they do. That is the American dream."

"Members of the jury," said J.R. firmly, "it is your duty as Americans to award Carrie Williams the full one hundred and twenty dollars that she earned."

Clifford stood silently for a moment, looking at the jurors. Then he said, "Thank you again for your attention," and sat down next to Carrie Williams, who gave him an encouraging smile.

"Mr. Streiby," said Judge Hoke, "it is your turn to make your argument."

C.O. Streiby stood, straightened his coat, and approached the jury box. He smiled broadly and spoke in a conversational manner.

"Members of the jury," said Streiby, "of course, I also ask you to follow the law. But the law does not contradict our common sense."

Streiby gripped the lapels of his coat and leaned toward the jury. "Now, we all know that no one may perform work and then just make a claim for payment—unless there is a contract to do the work!"

"Let's take an example that anyone can understand," Streiby said. Streiby shot a quick but pointed glance at J.R. and then continued: "Members of the jury, I cannot build a shed in your backyard in the middle of the night, and then in the morning present you with a bill, if you did not first agree to pay me."

Streiby pointed at Harold Meyer, who was doing his best to show a look of firm assurance.

"My client, the Board of Education," said Streiby, "set the term for the colored school at five months—and no one challenged the Board's action! So, Mrs. Williams cannot make her claim in this Court."

Streiby grasped the railing of the jury box with one hand. He raised his other arm and pointed his index finger at the jurors. "Members of the jury," Streiby declaimed loudly, "you must find for my client!" And with that, he pushed himself back from the jury box railing and returned to his table.

Harold Meyer stood up and shook Streiby's hand vigorously.

Judge Hoke rapped his gavel, and the two men sat down.

"Members of the Jury," Judge Hoke said, "the time has come for you to deliberate on your verdict. The audience will be silent while the jury leaves the room."

The courtroom audience was hushed. Led by the bailiff, the jurors rose from their seats and filed into the jury room, closing the door behind them.

Seated at the table, Carrie Williams spoke to J.R. in a low voice.

"What do you think, Mr. Clifford?" Carrie asked J.R. anxiously.

"How did we do? Will we win?"

"You did wonderfully, Mrs. Williams," said J.R. "I don't know if we shall be successful. And even if the jury's verdict is for you, the case may not be over. The School Board probably will appeal any judgment in our favor."

"But we do have a chance at winning, don't we?" asked Carrie.

"Of course we do, Mrs. Williams," said J.R. "After all, you followed the law."

There was a loud knock at the jury room door.

J.R. straightened in his chair. "Mrs. Williams," he said, "prepare yourself. I think that the jury may have already decided this case!"

The bailiff opened the door, and the jurors filed into the jury box. "Members of the jury," Judge Hoke asked, "have you reached a verdict?"

The jury foreman, who from his bib overalls looked to be a farmer, stood and faced the Judge.

"We have, your Honor," the foreman said. "We find for the plaintiff, Mrs. Carrie Williams, in the amount of $120.00."

There was a ripple of voices in the courtroom audience. Streiby and Meyer reacted with deep frowns. Carrie Williams and J.R. Clifford smiled broadly, and Abraham gave a shout of joy.

Judge Hoke rapped his gavel. "Order in the Court! Mr. Streiby, do you have any intentions regarding appeal?"

"Your Honor," said Streiby, "the Board of Education will naturally appeal this outrageous decision to the West Virginia Supreme Court!"

"Mr. Clifford, is there anything further for the Plaintiff?" asked the judge.

"Your Honor," J.R. said, "we will respond to any appeal, although we would prefer to simply collect the money that is due us."

"Very well," said Judge Hoke, "I will enter judgment for the Plaintiff, with interest at ten percent per annum. Mr. Clifford, it has been a pleasure to have you in our courtroom. You are indeed a credit to Storer College."

The Judge turned to the jurors. "Thank you for your service as jurors in this case. You are now excused. And, there being nothing further in this case, court is adjourned."

The judge banged his gavel a final time, and the bailiff, Judge, and jury left the courtroom.

Abraham rushed from his seat to Carrie's side. He hugged his wife with one arm, and with the other, he grasped J.R.'s hand, shaking it vigorously.

"Thank you so much, Mr. Clifford," Abraham said. "This is a great day for Tucker County—and for West Virginia!"

"You are most welcome, Mr. Williams," said J.R. "This jury did justice today. Now we must concentrate on persuading the Supreme Court judges that the law requires them to uphold the jury's verdict."

In the distance, a locomotive sounded its whistle. J.R. began sliding the papers from the table into his briefcase.

"Mr. and Mrs. Williams," he said, "I will write to you as soon as I receive the appeal papers. Now I must hurry to catch the next train up the Canyon. Tell those students in Coketon to study hard, Mrs. Williams!"

"I will," said Carrie. "I hope we will do well in the appeal."

"So do I, Mrs. Williams," said J.R. "So do I!"

J.R. picked up his briefcase, saluted Carrie and Abraham Williams, and hurried out of the courtroom.

CHAPTER FIVE

Martinsburg, West Virginia, 1913

In J.R. Clifford's parlor, Freda Clifford perched on a stool next to her great-uncle's chair and swung her legs excitedly.

"Wow, Uncle John!" she said, "That was an exciting trial! But why did the School Board think they could win an appeal?"

"Freda," said J.R., "the law in the 1890s was not friendly to colored people. The School Board hoped that the West Virginia Supreme Court would follow the lead of other states with segregated schools."

"Remember, Freda," said Carrie, "not everywhere in West Virginia was like Tucker County, where blacks and whites worked side by side."

"That's right," said J.R. "Racial discrimination was being upheld in courts all across the country. We certainly didn't know what to expect in an appeal."

"What happened?" asked Freda, her eyes shining with interest. "Did those mean men get taught a lesson?"

J.R. smiled at the irrepressible girl.

"Will you tell me about the appeal too, Uncle John?" asked Freda. "Pretty please?"

Carrie nodded her encouragement.

"I suppose I had better," said J.R. with a laugh, "or you will never stop asking!"

*   *   *   *   *

Charleston, West Virginia, 1898

The year was 1898. In the argument chambers of the West Virginia Supreme Court of Appeals in Charleston, long red velvet curtains glinted in the morning light, along the walls of the high-ceilinged courtroom.

Carrie and Abraham Williams sat on dark wooden chairs in the audience section. Carrie's lawyer, J.R. Clifford, sat at the front of the courtroom next to an ornate, carved podium. The podium faced a wide elevated bench. Four high-backed chairs sat behind the bench, facing the podium

C. O. Streiby, lawyer for the Tucker County School Board, was seated on the other side of the podium. In the courtroom audience, Streiby's client, School Board Secretary Harold Meyer, sat on another chair near Carrie and Abraham.

At the rear of the courtroom, newspapermen and lawyers joked with one another—until the bailiff announced loudly, "The Honorable, the Judges of the West Virginia Supreme Court of Appeals!"

The courtroom grew quiet. Four judges in black robes entered the room and sat down behind the bench.

Chief Judge Marmaduke Dent, his graying moustache reaching almost to his jawbone, sat in the far left chair. "Lawyer Streiby," said Judge Dent, "are you ready to make your argument?"

"I am, your Honor," said Streiby.

Streiby moved to the podium. He gave a relaxed smile to the judges.

"May it please the Court," Streiby said, "the principal point that I wish to make is that Mrs. Williams never had a contract with the Board to teach for eight months."

"In fact," he added, raising his eyebrows, "Teacher Williams refused to sign the contract that the Board prepared."

Judge Henry Brannon, sitting next to Judge Dent, had a grizzled beard and a balding head. "But Mr. Streiby," asked Judge Brannon, "was the Board's contract legal? It was only for five months. Should Teacher Williams have signed an illegal contract?"

"Your Honor," said Streiby, giving a respectful nod to the Judge, "I do not concede for an instant that the five-month contract was illegal."

"Well," continued Judge Brannon, "since she did not sign your contract, did Mrs. Williams have any contract for the five months that the Board did pay her for?"

'No," said Streiby, "she did not. As I said, she refused to sign."

"Then why did you pay Mrs. Williams at all?" asked Judge Brannon, furrowing his brow in seeming confusion. "What is the difference then whether Mrs. Williams had a written contract or not? She did the work."

"The difference," said Streiby, "is that the Board voted to pay her for only five months. Why, your Honors," he continued, "if we just let people do work without authorization and then demand payment, we shall not have a sound business climate in our young State!"

Sitting next to Judge Brannon was Judge Henry MacWhorter. His round rimless glasses and high collar made him look like a minister.

"What do you think of Teacher Williams' claim that having only five months school for the colored children is contrary to West Virginia law?" Judge MacWhorter asked.

"I do not think that this Court needs to decide that question in this case," Streiby replied, his tone defensive. "After all," said Streiby, "no one challenged the School Board vote at the time, which would have been the appropriate occasion."

Judge John W. English, at the other end of the bench, sported a wispy goatee. "Mr. Streiby," said Judge English, "I think that we do have to decide that question. After all, this Court's most important job is to interpret West Virginia law."

"The law says that colored and white shall have separate schools," Judge English stated simply. "The question that we must answer, it seems to me, is whether those separate schools must have the same terms or not?"

"I agree," said Judge MacWhorter. "Boards of Education across this state need to know their duty under the law. Can each School Board set whatever term they want? In some counties, they might only give the colored children two months."

"Your Honors," Streiby said, "I submit that the decision is best left to the discretion of each School Board. The local board knows their citizens, their finances, and the needs of their citizens."

In the courtroom audience, Harold Meyer nodded his head vigorously.

"Thank you, Mr. Streiby," said Judge Dent politely. "I believe we understand your case."

Streiby gathered his notes and stepped away from the podium.

"Now, Mr. Clifford," said Judge Dent, "it is your turn to make your argument."

J.R. moved to the podium, but he had no chance to deliver his prepared statement. Judge Henry Brannon fired off a question that went to the heart of Carrie Williams' case.

"Mr. Clifford," said Judge Brannon, "Mr. Streiby says that your client had no written contract to teach eight months, so she cannot be paid for eight months. What do you say to that?"

"I respectfully disagree with Mr. Streiby," J.R. said, his voice level and calm. "My client, Mrs. Carrie Williams, simply followed the law of this State. And of course Mrs. Williams would not sign an illegal contract."

Judge Brannon received J.R.'s answer with a thoughtful look, but did not reply—so J.R. continued his argument.

"Your Honors," J.R. said, "children in schools for white and colored must be treated equally, and the School Board must act in accordance with the law."

"Well, Mr. Clifford," asked Judge Dent, "what about the business climate in our young State? After all, contracts must be respected."

"Your Honor," said J.R., "I completely agree with you. This case is very important to West Virginia's business climate."

"Each year," he continued, "more and more colored people are being recruited to move to West Virginia, to work in our state's mines and mills. One of the great attractions of West Virginia is that here a hard-working, honest, black man can vote, and his children can get a decent education."

"A quality educational system for all children," J.R. said forcefully, "is good for West Virginia's business climate."

Judge English leaned forward. He had a serious expression on his face.

"Here's my concern, Mr. Clifford," Judge English said. "If we leave the length of the school term to each local School Board, what will happen?"

"Your Honor," J.R. said, "School Boards are often afraid to raise taxes. Colored children will not get an adequate education, and they will become a burden on society."

There was a pause. Then Judge Brannon spoke out of the silence.

"Mr. Clifford," said Judge Brannon thoughtfully, "this is not an easy case. If we rule in your client's favor, will our ruling solve the problems of race in our schools?"

"Respectfully, your Honor," said J.R., "as long as the notion of 'race' is used to divide and discriminate among our citizens, our nation's promise will not be fulfilled—not in our schools, and not anywhere else."

Looking for a moment at each judge, J.R. then spoke from his heart. "When I served in our nation's Army," he said, "I hoped that after the War, men and women would not be classified as 'colored' or 'white,' but simply as human beings. But those hopes have not yet come to pass."

"A decision for my client, Mrs. Carrie Williams," said J.R, "will not solve all of our state's racial problems. But a decision for Mrs. Williams will be a step in the right direction, bringing us closer to justice for all."

"Thank you, Mr. Clifford," said Judge Dent. "I believe we understand your position."

J.R. collected his papers from the podium and sat down.

Judge Dent

"Now the Court will deliberate," said Judge Dent. "We will return in a few minutes to announce our decision."

The four judges stood and filed out of the courtroom. J.R. stood up and walked to where Carrie and Abraham were sitting.

"Mr. Clifford," Carrie said, blinking back tears, "your argument was wonderful."

"I did nothing but speak the truth," said J.R. "It was you and Abraham who took a great risk, when you continued teaching for three months without pay."

Carrie's voice was full of emotion. "I knew we were right," she said.

"I wish that being right was enough," said J.R. "But we have been right for so long, and we are still enduring terrible discrimination. Who knows if our efforts will amount to anything?"

"Mr. Clifford," said Abraham, grasping J.R.'s hand, "those children in Coketon are the future. We are fighting for them, and we can never stop doing that."

"Amen to that, Mr. Williams," said J.R.

From the front of the courtroom a loud voice rang out. "All rise!" said the bailiff, "for the Judges of the West Virginia Supreme Court!"

The judges' dark robes swirled behind them as they re-entered the courtroom and took their seats.

Judge Dent stood, while the other judges looked out at the audience, their expressions serious. Judge Dent read from a long sheet of paper.

"We conclude that discrimination against the colored people, because of color alone, is contrary to public policy and the law of the land," Judge Dent read.

There were murmurs of surprise from the back of the room where the newspapermen were scribbling on their pads.

Judge Dent looked sternly at the audience. He continued reading: "If any discrimination in education should be made, it should be favorable to, and not against, the colored people."

As Judge Dent spoke, Harold Meyer's face darkened. Judge Dent continued to read from the Court's opinion:

"The Board of Education says in this case," he read, "that school terms of equal length would have cost more money for the colored children. But the law guaranteed colored pupils eight months of school, and even though it cost many times in proportion to what the white schools cost, they should have had it."

"We conclude," said the Judge, "that the judgment of the jury of twelve citizens in the Circuit Court of Tucker County, in favor of Carrie Williams, should be affirmed."

"There being nothing further in this case," Judge Dent concluded, "this Court is adjourned."

"All rise," said the bailiff. The courtroom audience rose, and the four judges stood and left the courtroom.

Carrie and Abraham Williams hurried to Mr. Clifford's side.

"We won!" said Carrie, clapping her hands together.

"Mrs. Williams," said J.R. with quiet awe in his voice, "this is an historic day." He grasped both of her hands. "For the first time in America," he said, "a court has ruled that school terms must be equal in white and colored schools."

From across the courtroom, where he had been consoling his client Harold Meyer, C.O. Streiby walked to where J.R. stood with his clients. Streiby extended his hand to J.R. The two lawyers shook hands.

"Mr. Clifford," Streiby said, "you presented a fine argument. Maybe those judges have a point after all."

Carrie Williams reached in front of J. R. and tapped C.O. Streiby on the arm. "Excuse me, Mr. Streiby," said Carrie. "Before you go off, I believe that this case is finally over—so what about my three months' pay?"

J.R. Clifford and Abraham Williams laughed. Carrie Williams was not afraid to speak up.

Streiby gave Carrie a courtly nod. "Mrs. Williams," he said, "we will have your payment for you within the week."

"Don't forget the interest!" Carrie Williams returned with a grin.

CHAPTER SIX

Martinsburg, West Virginia, 1913

The wind blew a fresh blaze of bright-colored leaves past J.R. Clifford's house in Martinsburg. Inside, Freda clapped her hands and danced a few steps around the floor.

"That was great, Uncle John!" she said. "You and Mrs. Williams won a great victory! But is Mrs. Williams' case still part of our West Virginia law?"

"Yes, Freda, it is." said J.R. "And, because of the Williams case, your school term must be just as long as the white children's term."

"Oh—I'm not sure I like that," said Freda with a playful pout.

"Yes, you do, Freda!" said J. R, wagging his finger.

"Not only that, Mr. Clifford," said Carrie Williams. "Because of our case, my daughter Clara will have the same salary at Sumner School as the teachers in the white schools."

"West Virginia can attract well-qualified colored teachers," Carrie explained further, "because teacher salaries here are better than in other states. Our case did that, too."

"Now, Mr. Clifford," she continued, "answer me a question. I know our case was an important victory. But when will we ever get rid of separate schools for colored children? They are just wrong."

"That's a very good question," said J.R. "We were just beginning our legal struggle with your case. Today, Howard University Law School is training black lawyers to bring cases in courts across the nation, challenging segregated schools. I'm hoping those cases will be successful."

J.R. picked up a framed photograph of a young woman from the table beside his chair. Next to the photo were a series of printed paragraphs. "Mrs. Williams," he said, "this is a picture taken at the Niagara Movement meeting at Harpers Ferry, back in 1906."

"Is Niagara where everyone took off their shoes?" asked Freda.

J.R. and Carrie smiled.

J.R. Clifford & W.E.B Dubois (front) at Niagara Movement, Harpers Ferry, West Virginia

"Yes, Freda," J.R. said, "we Niagara delegates removed our shoes, as a sign of respect, when we visited John Brown's Fort."

Freda tugged at her great-uncle's sleeve. "What did Aunt Mary do at the Niagara meeting?"

"I was so proud of Mary," said J.R. "She was just sixteen. She read the great 'Credo', written by my dear friend Dr. William E.B. DuBois." He handed the framed photo to Carrie Williams. "Mrs. Williams, the text of the 'Credo' is right there on the back of the frame. Won't you read some it for Freda?"

Carrie took the picture from J.R. "I believe in God," she read, "who made of one blood all races that dwell on earth." Carrie's voice was as strong and precise as it had been in the Tucker County courtroom, more than thirty years earlier.

"I believe that all men, black and brown, and white, are brothers, varying, through Time and Opportunity, in form and gift and feature, but differing in no essential particular, and alike in soul and in the possibility of infinite development."

Carrie handed the paper back to J.R. "Here, Mr. Clifford," she said, "you read a passage."

J.R. bent his head forward, to see the words more clearly. Then he straightened and read in a loud voice, as if he was addressing a courtroom:

"I believe in Liberty for all men; the space to stretch their arms and their souls; the right to breathe and the right to vote, the freedom to choose their friends, enjoy the sunshine and ride on the railroads, uncursed by color; thinking, dreaming, working as they will in a kingdom of God and love."

J.R. placed the frame back on the table, and looked fondly at his niece. "Freda," he asked, "did you like that?"

"Yes, Uncle John, I did," she said—her expression was serious.

"The spirit of the Niagara Movement will triumph," said J.R. "We will overcome segregation and the hateful legacy of slavery, Freda—and it's going to be up to your generation to continue our struggle."

Freda rose from her stool and shook her small fist in the air. "I'll do it, Uncle John. I will!" she said. "And I want to go in bare feet, too!"

"Of course you will, Freda," said Carrie, smiling. "You will make your Uncle John and Aunt Mary proud of you."

The three sat in silence for a moment. Then J.R. took a deep breath, and exhaled slowly.

"Mrs. Williams," J.R. said, "it has been a joy to see you, but I must rest now. I just can't talk for as long as I used to. Will you please call on me the next time you are in Martinsburg?"

Carrie Williams stood up and took J.R.'s hand. She gave him a loving look. "Thank you, Mr. Clifford, for having me as your guest."

Carrie walked to the doorway and turned to face J.R. She knew that this might the last time she would see this man who had meant so much in her life, and in the life of her people.

"Mr. Clifford," asked Carrie, "if someone, someday, in the distant future, were to read that transcript, and learn about our case, what will they think?"

J.R.'s fingers tapped the papers in his lap. He thought for a moment and then replied.

"Maybe, Mrs. Williams," J.R. said, "— maybe, they will sense that we were motivated by love for our people—and by determination to see that justice is done."

"I like that thought, Mr. Clifford," Carrie said.

"Goodbye, Mrs. Williams," said J.R.

"Goodbye," said Carrie, and she walked out of the parlor.

J.R. sat looking at the transcript in his lap. After a minute, he closed his eyes. Freda quietly slipped into the kitchen to put the lemonade away.

The choir next door sang, "I have seen Him in the watch-fires of a hundred circling camps . . . Glory, glory, hallelujah!"

J.R.'s head leaned forward until his chin rested on his chest.

The choir sang, "His Truth is marching on!"

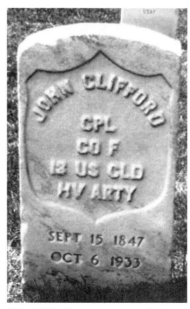

J.R. Clifford's gravestone at Arlington National Cemetery (Birth year should be 1848.)

APPENDICES

HISTORICAL ACCURACY, SOURCES AND CREDITS

The stories "A New Home for Liberty" and "J.R. Clifford and the Carrie Williams Case" span almost one hundred years—from pre-Civil War Virginia to West Virginia in 1933. The stories are about real historical events and real people, portrayed as accurately as possible. Where the historical record is silent, the stories rely on imagination; but the imagined events are in most cases at least possible.

Here are some examples of how these stories combine history and imagination.

In "A New Home for Liberty," the 1913 railroad station meeting between J.R. Clifford and Granville Hall is imagined, but it fits the facts. In that year, a newspaper reported that J.R. Clifford, then a prominent attorney, publisher, and political leader in West Virginia's African American community, had traveled to Parkersburg for a Republican Party event.

In the same time period, Granville Hall, by then a retired railroad executive, traveled to visit family in the Parkersburg area and to promote his books about West Virginia's founding. Passenger trains in West Virginia were not racially segregated (although they were next door in Virginia.)

If these two heroic West Virginians did not actually meet in 1913 and exchange their stories on the fiftieth anniversary of the State that they helped create and nurture, we think they would welcome the chance that our imagination can provide!

As to Granville Hall's and J.R. Clifford's childhoods, court and newspaper records show that Hall's father was indicted by the Harrison County (Virginia) grand jury for receiving and circulating antislavery newspapers, and he had to leave the State for a period of time.

Court records also show that free black farmers in the South Branch Valley like J.R. Clifford's parents helped many escaping slaves. J.R. Clifford wrote in his newspaper about his pride in joining the Union Army in Chicago; and Frederick Douglass' "Call to Arms" was widely printed at the time J.R. enlisted.

The dialogue in the Wheeling Statehood Convention scenes is compiled from official records kept by Granville Hall; and from the writings of Captain Gordon Battelle, Governor Francis Pierpont, and President Abraham Lincoln. Captain Battelle did die in an army camp while serving as a Union chaplain.

In the story "J.R. Clifford and the Carrie Williams Case," J.R. Clifford's 1892 visit to the Coketon Colored School is unrecorded by history, but the visit is more than plausible. One of J.R.'s relatives worked in Coketon, and Carrie Williams did testify in court that she had consulted with J.R. before she kept on teaching without pay.

The jury trial scene in this story is adapted from the original trial transcript. The dialogue in the appeal scene is based on the written arguments that the lawyers Clifford and Streiby filed with the Supreme Court of Appeals. The Supreme Court judges in the story are the real people who ruled for Carrie Williams and her pupils. Their legal opinion, printed in this volume, is still part of West Virginia law.

Sometime after 1900, Carrie Williams moved from Tucker County to Chicago, Illinois. Carrie's 1933 meeting in Martinsburg with J.R. and his niece Freda is imagined, but it is plausible that J.R. and Carrie stayed in touch and met after her case was over.

Freda Clifford (Rolls), a real person, was born near J.R.'s home place in 1925; she died in 2014. Freda remembered visiting with her famous "Uncle John," and she attended several J.R. Clifford Project events, where she was portrayed—accurately, we believe—as a precocious and feisty 9-year-old.

The stories "A New Home for Liberty" and "J.R. Clifford and the Carrie Williams Case" are both based on community dramatic programs, written by Thomas Rodd, that have been presented by the J.R. Clifford Project to audiences in West Virginia since 2004. The Project is administered by Friends of Blackwater, whose executive director is Judith Schoyer Rodd.

Senior West Virginia Supreme Court Justice Larry Starcher and attorney Katherine E. Dooley, Esq. have been long-term collaborators in the Project. Brandae Mullins, Lorraine Weaver, Valerie Little, Julie Palas, Megan Lowe, Sharon Harms, and David Vago made major creative contributions to the Project's programs. The historians Connie Park Rice, John Alexander Williams, and John E. Stealey III provided essential information and inspiration. Many of the dramatic and descriptive elements in the stories originated with the author's daughter, the writer and schoolteacher Priscilla Rodd. Ms. Colbert's West Virginia Studies class at Charles Town Middle School made valuable last-minute suggestions.

Thanks to these people and to hundreds of others too numerous to name individually whose participation, creativity, and enthusiasm has made the J.R. Clifford Project a successful and rewarding enterprise.

The J.R. Clifford Project has received financial support from many generous sources, including the West Virginia Supreme Court of Appeals, the West Virginia Legislature's Community Participation Program, the West Virginia Secretary for Arts and Education, the West Virginia Humanities Council, the Mountain State Bar, the West Virginia Bar Foundation, AT&T, the West Virginia University College of Law, the West Virginia University Libraries, the Appalachian Community Fund, the West Virginia Education Association Foundation, and numerous individual donors. Thanks to all!

Tom Rodd

Appendices

QUESTIONS FOR CRITICAL THINKING AND DISCUSSION

"A New Home for Liberty"

1. Why do you think there was a law in Virginia against reading anti-slavery newspapers? Why do you think Granville Hall's parents were reading anti-slavery newspapers, even though it meant breaking the law?

2. How do you think J.R. Clifford's parents felt when they learned that J.R. had enlisted in the Union Army? What might they have wished him to do instead, and why?

3. If you were a slave, do you think you would try to escape? Why or why not?

3. Why do you think that some delegates at the Wheeling Convention wanted to keep slavery in the new state? Why do you think their view did not succeed?

4. Why do you think African Americans in West Virginia were able to continue to vote after the Civil War, when that right was taken away in many other Southern states?

5. How do you think the Civil War improved life for African Americans? In what ways did it fail to improve their lives? Why?

"J.R. Clifford and the Carrie Williams Case"

1. Why do you think Carrie Williams decided to sue the Tucker County school board? What risks did she take when she worked past the date the Board set as the end of her teaching contract?

2. Were you surprised by the jury's verdict for Carrie Williams? Why do you think the jury decided the case in her favor?

3. What personal qualities did J.R. Clifford and Carrie Williams show in the story that you think helped them win their case, and why did those qualities help?

4. What do you think was J.R. Clifford's best argument in the Supreme Court appeal, and why? What do you think was C.O. Streiby's best argument, and why?

5. Why do you think the Supreme Court ruled for Carrie Williams?

Appendices

WORDS AND TERMS

abolitionist – a person who is opposed to slavery, and who wants people who are slaves to obtain liberty and freedom.

appeal – asking a higher court to change or reverse the decision of a lower court.

bailiff – a police officer who helps the judge in a courtroom.

coke ovens – brick ovens where coal is partially burned by allowing very little air to get to the fire. The coal changes into a more pure substance called "coke," that is used to make iron and steel.

constitution – a written document that sets the basic rules and laws for a state or nation—as in "the West Virginia Constitution" or "the United States Constitution."

contract – an agreement that can be enforced in a court, usually written.

delegate – a person at a meeting who represents a certain area or group—as in "the delegate from Kanawha County."

emancipation – changing from being a slave to being a free person.

enlist – to join an army.

liberty – freedom; enjoying the basic rights of a citizen of a state or nation.

racial discrimination – treating people differently because of their appearance or who their ancestors were.

segregation – a system of racial separation and discrimination used in many states after the Civil War.

slavery – a system where one person (the "master") can legally own (and control, restrain, punish, and/or sell) another person (the "slave")—and the slave's children.

statehood – adding a new state to the United States of America. The USA started with thirteen states and now has fifty. West Virginia was the thirty-fifth state added to the Union.

Supreme Court of Appeals – in West Virginia, the highest court, where decisions from lower courts can be reviewed.

transcript – a written record of what is said in a court, often taken down by a special "court reporter."

verdict – the decision of a court after a trial, often made by a jury.

Wheeling Convention – a series of meetings in the City of Wheeling beginning in April of 1861 and ending in July of 1863, for the purpose of creating the new State of West Virginia from part of Virginia.

TIMELINE OF EVENTS IN THE LIFE OF J.R. CLIFFORD

1848 – John Robert "J.R." Clifford, the son of Isaac and Satilpa Kent Clifford, was born on September 13 at Williamsport, then a town in Virginia and now in Grant County, West Virginia near the Town of Moorefield. (The date is incorrect on J.R.'s Arlington gravestone.)

1864 – J.R. enlisted in the Union Army andwas assigned to the 13th Regiment, U.S. Heavy Artillery, Company F, United States Colored Troops, organized at Camp Nelson, Kentucky. He mustered out in November of 1865.

1873 – After working for several years as a barber and teaching in "writing schools" in Ohio and West Virginia, J.R. enrolled at Storer College in Harpers Ferry, West Virginia, where he graduated in 1875.

1875-85 – J.R. served as a teacher and then as principal at Sumner School in Martinsburg, West Virginia. John W. Cromwell wrote in the Journal of Negro History, Vol. 8, No. 3, July 1923. "I attended a Teacher's Institute . . . held at Harper's Ferry, in 1877. There I first saw a gathering of young teachers, vigorous and alert, none more chivalric in bearing than the central figure in the person of John R. Clifford, at that time Principal of the Grammar School at Martinsburg. He helped to shoot off the shackles from four million slaves and cement this Union on the bloody battle fields during the war of the sixties and holds an honorable discharge in proof of it."

1876 – J.R. married Mary Franklin, whom he met at Storer College.

1882 – J.R. founded The Pioneer Press, which he edited and published until 1917.

1887 – J.R. passed the bar exam and was admitted to practice before the West Virginia Supreme Court of Appeals, becoming West Virginia's first African American lawyer. He practiced law in Martinsburg, West Virginia until his death in 1933.

1898 – The West Virginia Supreme Court issued its opinion in Carrie Williams vs. the Tucker County Board of Education. The Williams case was a first in American jurisprudence and played an important role in establishing West Virginia as a state where African Americans could exercise political and economic power.

1906 – J.R. helped his friend W.E.B. DuBois organize the first American meeting of the Niagara Movement at Harpers Ferry, West Virginia. The Niagara Movement was the precursor of the National Association for the Advancement of Colored People and the cornerstone of the 20th Century civil rights movement.

1933 – J.R. Clifford died on October 6, 1933 at the age of 85 and was buried in Mt. Hope Cemetery, Martinsburg, West Virginia. He and his wife were reburied at Arlington National Cemetery in 1954.

TIMELINE OF WEST VIRGINIA STATEHOOD

April 17, 1861 – A majority of the Virginia legislature approves secession from the United States.

May 13, 1861 – Pro-Union leaders in Northwest Virginia summon First Wheeling Convention.

June 11, 1861 – Second Wheeling Convention begins, and creates a new Virginia state government that is loyal to the Union.

July 11, 1861 – In the Battle of Rich Mountain, the Union Army pushes Confederates from the Northwest Virginia region.

November 26, 1861 – The West Virginia Constitutional Convention begins meeting in Wheeling, to form a new state out of part of Virginia.

May 13, 1862 – The loyal government in Wheeling completes the state-making process and submits a new state constitution that does not mention slavery to Congress.

December 31, 1862 – President Lincoln signs a bill passed by Congress creating West Virginia but requiring the gradual abolition of slavery in the new state.

March 26, 1863 – the West Virginia Constitution is amended as required by Congress.

June 20, 1863 – West Virginia enters the Union as the 35th state.

February 3, 1865 – slavery was officially abolished by the West Virginia Legislature.

TEXT OF THE WEST VIRGINIA SUPREME COURT OPINION IN THE CARRIE WILLIAMS CASE

In the Supreme Court of Appeals of West Virginia.
WILLIAMS v. BOARD OF EDUCATION OF FAIRFAX DISTRICT.
Nov. 16, 1898.
31 S.E. 985, 45 W.Va. 199

Syllabus by the Court.

1. The law of this state does not authorize boards of education to discriminate between white and colored schools in the same district as to length of term to be taught.

2. Where a teacher has been employed to teach a colored school by the trustees thereof, under the supervision of the board of education, and she teaches the same the full term of the other primary schools in the same district, satisfactorily to the patrons of such school, she is entitled to pay for her whole term of service; and the board of education cannot escape the payment thereof by interposing a plea that it had, by reason of the school being a colored school, limited the term thereof to a shorter period than the white schools in the same district. Such discrimination, being made merely on account of color, cannot be recognized or tolerated, as it is contrary to public policy and the law of the land.

Error to Circuit Court, Tucker County; Joseph T. Hoke, Judge.

Action by Carrie Williams against the Board of Education of Fairfax District, in the County of Tucker. Judgment for plaintiff, and defendant brings error. Affirmed.

C. O. Strieby, for plaintiff in error.

J. R. Clifford and A. G. Dayton, for defendant in error.

DENT, J.

Carrie Williams sues the board of education of Fairfax district, in the county of Tucker, for three months' unpaid services as teacher of the colored school of Coketon, in said district, amounting to $120, and also $1 deducted illegally off of a previous month's salary for failure to return the term report required by law. The circuit court gave her judgment, and the board brings the matter to this court, and now here interposes the following defenses:

1. That the individual names of the members of the board are set out in the summons and declaration. This was wholly unnecessary, and will be regarded as mere surplusage.

2. That her appointment as a teacher was not in writing, as required by section 13, c. 45, Code. After the service has been rendered in a satisfactory manner to the patrons of the school, and the board has recognized and approved it by receiving her monthly reports, and paying her five months' salary, it is too late for them to object that her appointment was not in writing, as required by law.

3. That the trustees had not established a primary school as required by section 17, c. 45, Code, the enumeration of colored children being 26, but had apportioned the funds under section 18, Id., assigning to the colored children their pro rata share. This is directly in the face of the positive mandatory requirement of the statute, and it is contrary to public policy to entertain such a plea. No public officer should be permitted to plead his own misconduct in defense of what would otherwise be a just legal claim against him. On the contrary, the court will presume that he faithfully discharged the duties of his office,

in the very face of his plea, when such presumption appears proper. In this case the trustees established a colored school at Coketon; and it must be presumed that this was done in accordance with the provisions of section 17, and not section 18, c. 45, Code. To hold otherwise would be to condemn the trustees as guilty of a plain failure of duty, subjecting them to the penalties imposed by section 59 of said chapter, which would be unjust to them in the face of the matters contained in the record. The trustees are not parties in any wise to this suit, and it is hardly fair to them for the board to seek to defend itself by alleging neglect of plain mandatory duty on their part, if legally proper to do so, which is certainly not the law.

4. That, the people of the district having voted for an eight months' school, the board arbitrarily determined the white schools should run eight months, and the colored school only five months. This distinction on the part of the board, being clearly illegal, and a discrimination made merely on account of color, should be treated as a nullity, as being contrary to public policy and good morals. At the end of five months the board notified the teacher to stop the school, the only reason for so doing being their discriminating action towards the colored school. This she refused to do, but taught it, satisfactorily to the patrons of the school, the full eight months authorized by law. In the case of West Virginia Transp. Co. v. Ohio River Pipe-Line Co., 22 W. Va. 617, it is said: "The common law will not permit individuals to oblige themselves by a contract either to do or not to do anything when the thing to be done or omitted is in any degree clearly injurious to the public." On page 3 of Greenhood on Public Policy it is said: "The element of public policy in the law of contracts and in the law generally is by no means of recent origin, but owes its existence to the very sources from which our common law is supplied." "It secures the people against the corruption of justice or the public service, and places itself as a barrier before all devices

to disregard public convenience." And on page 3: "By 'public policy' is intended that principle of the law which holds that no subject can lawfully do that which has a tendency to be injurious to the public or the public good." Hence no court will permit an otherwise just claim to be defended on the grounds of dereliction of duty or misconduct on the part of any public officer, because detrimental to the public service, and injurious to the common weal. As no individual can take advantage of his own wrong, so no public servant can take advantage of his own illegal conduct, or failure to discharge his official duties in accordance with the express provisions of the statute that creates him. Ignorance of law is no excuse, and violation of law is no defense. Discrimination against the colored people, because of color alone, as to privileges, immunities, and equal legal protection, is contrary to public policy and the law of the land. If any discrimination as to education should be made, it should be favorable to, and not against, the colored people. Held in the bondage of slavery, and continued in a low moral and intellectual condition, for a long period of years, and then clothed at once, without preparation, with full citizenship, in this great republic, and the power to control and guide its destinies, the future welfare, prosperity, and peace of our people demand that this benighted race should be elevated by education, both morally and intellectually, that they may become exemplary citizens; otherwise the perpetuity of our free institutions may be greatly endangered.

The board claims, however, that the proper remedy was by mandamus, and that the plaintiff had no right to take the law into her own hands. How much better was it for the patrons of the school, the board, and the public, that she should regard her employment as strictly in accordance with law, and disregard the illegal discrimination on account of color, and thus secure to her pupils their legal rights, without resort to the writ of mandamus, which, while it might have condemned and punished the board, would have been inadequate to furnish the relief sought. There is no question that she was employed to teach the school, and that she did teach it in accordance with law, and satisfactorily to its patrons. But the board says, it being a colored school, it was allowed its pro rata share of the funds, and limited to the period of five months. This action on its part, being without authority, and in direct disobedience of law, must be disregarded, and the board presumed to have discharged its legal duties.

Counsel insist that the colored pupils, having been allotted their pro rata share of the school funds, have no right to complain. The law guaranteed them eight months of school, and, though it cost many times in proportion what the white schools cost, they should have had it. Money values should not be set off against moral and intellectual improvement. A nation that depends on its wealth is a depraved nation, while moral purity and intellectual progress alone can preserve the integrity of free institutions, and the love of true liberty, under the protection of equal laws, in the hearts of the people. The judgment is affirmed.

ABRAHAM LINCOLN ON THE ADMISSION OF WEST VIRGINIA

December 31, 1862

THE CONSENT of the Legislature of Virginia is constitutionally necessary to the bill for the admission of West Virginia becoming a law. A body claiming to be such Legislature has given its consent. We cannot well deny that it is such, unless we do so upon the outside knowledge that the body was chosen at elections, in which a majority of the qualified voters of Virginia did not participate. But it is a universal practice in the popular elections in all these States to give no legal consideration whatever to those who do not choose to vote, as against the effect of the votes of those who do choose to vote. Hence it is not the qualified voters, but the qualified voters, who choose to vote, that constitute the political power of the State. Much less than to non-voters, should any consideration be given to those who did not vote, in this case: because it is also a matter of outside knowledge, that they were not merely neglectful of their rights under, and duty to, this government, but were also engaged in open rebellion against it. Doubtless among these non-voters were some Union men whose voices were smothered by the more numerous secessionists; but we know too little of their number to assign them any appreciable value. Can the government stand, if it indulges Constitutional constructions by which men in open rebellion against it, are to be accounted, man for man, the equals of those who maintain their loyalty to it? Are they to be accounted even better citizens, and more worthy of consideration, than those who merely neglect to vote? If so, their treason against the Constitution, enhances their constitutional value! Without braving these absurd conclusions, we cannot deny that the body which consents to the admission of West Virginia, is the Legislature of Virginia.

I do not think the plural form of the words "Legislatures" and "States" in the phrase of the Constitution "without the consent of the Legislatures of the States concerned" has any reference to the new State concerned. That plural form sprang from the contemplation of two or more old States, contributing to form a new one. The idea that the new state was in danger of being admitted without its own consent, was not provided against, because it was not thought of, as I conceive. It is said, the devil takes care of his own. Much more should a good spirit - the spirit of the Constitution and the Union - take care of its own. I think it cannot do less, and live.

But is the admission into the Union, of West Virginia, expedient. This, in my general view, is more a question for Congress, than for the Executive. Still I do not evade it. More than on anything else, it depends on whether the admission or rejection of the new State would, under all the circumstances tend the more strongly to the restoration of the National authority throughout the Union. That which helps most in this direction is most expedient at this time. Doubtless those in remaining Virginia would return to the Union, so to speak, less reluctantly without the division of the old state than with it; but I think we could not save as much in this quarter by rejecting the new state, as we should lose by it in West Virginia. We can scarcely dispense with the aid of West Virginia in this struggle; much less can we afford to have her against us, in Congress and in the field. Her brave and good men regard her admission into the Union as a matter of life and death. They have been true to the Union under very severe trials. We have so acted as to justify their hopes; and we cannot fully retain their confidence, and co-operation, if we seem to break faith with them. In fact, they could not do so much for us, if they would.

Again, the admission of the new State turns that much slave soil to free; and thus, is a certain, and irrevocable encroachment upon the cause of the rebellion.

The division of a State is dreaded as a precedent. But a measure made expedient by a war, is no precedent for times of peace. It is said the admission of West Virginia is secession, and tolerated only because it is our secession. Well, if we can call it by that name, there is still difference enough between secession against the Constitution, and secession in favor of the Constitution.

I believe the admission of West Virginia into the Union is expedient.

- Abraham Lincoln
December 31, 1862, Lincoln Papers, Library of Congress.

BIBLIOGRAPHY

Sources about J.R. Clifford and the Carrie Williams case

"A Timeline of African-American History in West Virginia," West Virginia Archives and History.

http://www.wvculture.org/history/timeline.html

Medals awarded to African American Union Civil War soldiers by West Virginia, compiled by Linda Cunningham Fluharty.

http://www.lindapages.com/45/cw-45us.htm

"For Men and Measures: The Life and Legacy of Civil Rights Pioneer, J.R. Clifford," Connie Park Rice, 2007 PhD. thesis, West Virginia University.

http://wvuscholar.wvu.edu:8881//exlibris/dtl/d3_1/apache_media/L2V4bGlcmlzL2R0bC9kM18xL2FwYWNoZV9tZWRpYS8xMzU4Mg==.pdf

Selected stories from J.R. Clifford's newspaper, The Pioneer Press.

http://www.jrclifford.org/images/PioneerPressCentEdition.pdf

Compilation of articles about J.R. Clifford, 2006 Niagara Movement Centennial

http://www.jrclifford.org/The%20Pioneer%20Press.htm

Arlington National Cemetery, "John Robert Clifford."

http://www.arlingtoncemetery.net/jrclifford.htm

Website of the J.R. Clifford Project, Charleston, WV.
http://www.jrclifford.org"www.jrclifford.org

"J.R. Clifford," West Virginia Archives and History.
http://www.wvculture.org/history/clifford.html

Reid, John Phillip, "An American Judge -- Marmaduke Dent of West Virginia," New York University Press, New York (1968)

Lewis, Ronald L. "Marmaduke Dent." e-WV: The West Virginia Encyclopedia. 16 October 2012.
http://www.wvencyclopedia.org/articles/1882

"Storer College," National Park Service, Harper's Ferry National Historical Park
http://www.nps.gov/hafe/learn/historyculture/upload/Storer%20College.pdf

Sources about West Virginia statehood, Granville Hall, and Gordon Battelle

"Road to Statehood: Timeline to Statehood," West Virginia Public Broadcasting, lesson plan with images, source links, and exercises.
http://d43fweuh3sg51.cloudfront.net/media/media_files/road-to-statehood-timeline.pdf

"First and Second Wheeling Conventions: The Constitution of 1861-63," the West Virginia Online Encyclopedia.

98

http://www.wvhumanities.org/Statehood/secondwheeling-convention.htm

Index to Statehood Primary Documents, "A State of Convenience – the Creation of West Virginia," West Virginia Archives and History.

http://www.wvculture.org/history/statehood/primarydocuments.html

"Timeline of West Virginia: Civil War and Statehood," West Virginia Archives and History

http://www.wvculture.org/history/sesquicentennial/timeline.html

Williams, John Alexander "Formation of West Virginia." e-WV: The West Virginia Encyclopedia. 14 October 2013.

http://www.wvencyclopedia.org/articles/2034

"Lincoln and the 'Vast Question' of West Virginia," Dallas S. Shaffer, West Virginia History, Volume 32, Number 2 (January 1971), pp. 86-100.

http://www.wvculture.org/history/journal_wvh/wvh32-2.html

"The Rending of Virginia," Granville Hall, first published in 1902, reprinted by University of Tennessee Press, Knoxville, 2000; biographical introduction by Dr. John E. Stealey III.

http://newfoundpress.utk.edu/pubs/hall/frontmatter.pdf

Stealey III, John Edmund "The Rending of Virginia." e-WV: The West Virginia Encyclopedia. 02 November 2012.

http://www.wvencyclopedia.org/articles/58

Biographical sketch and obituary of Gordon Battelle, Linda Cunningham Fluharty.
http://www.lindapages.com/wvcw/1wvi/1wvi-battelle.htm

"Gordon Battelle," the West Virginia Online Encyclopedia.
http://www.wvencyclopedia.org/articles/406

"Gordon Battelle's Plea for a Free State," Chapter 16, "The Rending of Virginia," Granville Hall, University of Tennessee Press, Knoxville, 2000.
http://newfoundpress.utk.edu/pubs/hall/chp16.pdf

ABOUT THE AUTHOR

Thomas Whitney Rodd, born in 1946 in Pittsburgh, Pennsylvania, is a retired West Virginia attorney. He attended Berea College and Fairmont State College, graduated from West Virginia University Law School, and lives in Preston County, West Virginia.